1st EDITION

Perspectives on Diseases and Disorders

Eating Disorders

Lorraine Savage

Editor

Other books is this series:

AIDS
Autism
Cancer
Diabetes
Obesity

1st EDITION

Perspectives on Diseases and Disorders

Eating Disorders

Lorraine Savage
Editor

Detroit • New York • San Francisco • New Haven, Conn. • Waterville, Maine • London

LIBRARY OF CONGRESS CATALOGING-IN-PUBLICATION DATA

Eating disorders / Lorraine Savage, book editor.
    p. cm. — (Perspectives on diseases and disorders)
Includes bibliographical references and index.
ISBN-13: 978-0-7377-3872-8 (hardcover)
1. Eating disorders—Popular works. I. Savage, Lorraine.
RC552.E18E28211312 2008
362.196'8526--dc22   2007037455

ISBN-10: 0-7377-3872-3

Printed in the United States of America

CONTENTS

INTRODUCTION

For years, doctors, sociologists, and psychologists have debated the cause of eating disorders such as anorexia nervosa and bulimia. The generally held view was that eating disorders were mental illnesses that caused a young person, usually a woman, to try to gain control over her body by controlling what and when she ate. However, new studies into the human genome have revealed a physiological link between biology and eating disorders.

In an article in *Forbes* magazine, Walter Kaye, a researcher at the University of Pittsburgh studying anorexia, explains that researchers are discovering that the causes of eating disorders are physical rather than mental. "With anorexia, we're where schizophrenia or autism were 20 years ago." Kaye's point is that, like eating disorders, people once blamed autism and schizophrenia on upbringing and other social factors, but now scientists know that these disorders have physical causes. In recent years, numerous scientific studies have found a genetic link to the risk of developing eating disorders.

At the University of Pennsylvania Department of Psychiatry, researchers conducted tests on twins and families with a history of anorexia. People who were related to one another had a higher incidence of eating disorders than people who were unrelated. Interested in this phenomenon, researchers discovered a biological link on chromosome 1 that indicated heredity plays a role in the development of eating disorders.

Kelly Klump, an associate professor of psychology at Michigan State University, conducted genetic studies on five hundred fourteen-year-old female twins. Klump found that social factors were the primary cause of eating disorders in prepubescent girls, but after a girl has her first menstrual period, genetic factors were more likely to be the primary cause. These findings complemented Klump's earlier research that showed that girls age eleven had no genetic influences on their eating disorders, while girls age seventeen exhibited hereditary disordered eating patterns. Puberty, therefore, had a dramatic impact on the girls' susceptibility.

In another case, researchers at the Maudsley Hospital in London focused on the neurotransmitter serotonin, which regulates appetite and may contribute to anxiety. Researchers who studied the 5HT2A receptor in patients with anorexia found variations in the gene for serotonin. Women with eating disorders were twice as likely to have the variant gene as women who did not suffer from an eating disorder. The finding suggests that an increase in serotonin levels can contribute to a person's susceptibility of acquiring anorexia.

Dr. Cynthia M. Bulik, who has led a major study on the genetic link to eating disorders, says that heredity can contribute as much as 56 percent to susceptibility, with social and environmental factors as the remaining causes.

According to the National Alliance on Mental Illness, anorexia sufferers tend to have higher-than-normal levels of the brain hormone cortisol, which reacts to stress, and vasopressin, a chemical in people with obsessive-compulsive disorder. But while a genetic link has been found that can explain anorexia, the debate continues as to whether binge eating and obesity also have genetic causes.

Genetics and biochemical imbalances can partially explain binge eating. Obesity is hereditary, as the condition is clearly found among people who are related to one another. Metabolism and the ability to break down food and generate energy varies widely in people. Moreover, a problem in the hypothalamus region of the brain,

A healthy, well-balanced meal can sometimes be hard to stomach.
(AP Images)

which controls hunger signals, can lead to binge eating or other eating disorders.

Hormonal mechanisms that control hunger, such as leptin and ghrelin, also can affect obesity. For example, leptin-deficient and leptin-resistant people can suffer from binge eating. Some rare genetic abnormalities, such as Prader-Willi syndrome, predispose some people to obesity.

As scientists learn more about the human genome and its relationship to disease, no doubt other discoveries that relate mental illness to physical causes will develop. This relationship is certainly changing the way eating disorders are diagnosed and treated.

CHAPTER 1

An Overview of Eating Disorders

Symptoms, Causes, and Treatments of Eating Disorders

Melissa Spearing

According to Melissa Spearing of the National Institute of Mental Health, eating disorders such as anorexia nervosa, bulimia, and binge eating are medical illnesses. Spearing explains, however, that treatment is available and is successful if administered early after the onset of the disease. People with anorexia reduce their food intake to dangerous levels, leaving them malnourished and at risk for cardiac arrest and death. Bulimia patients binge eat then purge the food by vomiting or abusing laxatives. Binge eaters eat large amounts of food but do not purge, then feel disgusted or depressed by their actions. Treatment for sufferers of eating disorders usually covers monitoring, psychosocial intervention, and nutritional counseling to return the person to a healthy weight. Melissa Spearing works in the Public Information and Communications branch of the National Institute of Mental Health.

Photo on previous page. Neglecting nutritional needs is a contributing factor to the development of eating disorders. (AP Images)

Eating is controlled by many factors, including appetite, food availability, family, peer, and cultural practices, and attempts at voluntary control. Diet-

SOURCE: Melissa Spearing, "Eating Disorders: Facts About Eating Disorders and the Search for Solution," National Institute of Mental Health, 2001.

ing to a body weight leaner than needed for health is highly promoted by current fashion trends, sales campaigns for special foods, and in some activities and professions. *Eating disorders* involve serious disturbances in eating behavior, such as extreme and unhealthy reduction of food intake or severe overeating, as well as feelings of distress or extreme concern about body shape or weight. Researchers are investigating how and why initially voluntary behaviors, such as eating smaller or larger amounts of food than usual, at some point move beyond control in some people and develop into an eating disorder. Studies on the basic biology of appetite control and its alteration by prolonged overeating or starvation have uncovered enormous complexity, but in the long run have the potential to lead to new pharmacologic treatments for eating disorders.

Eating Disorders Are Treatable Medical Illnesses

Eating disorders are not due to a failure of will or behavior; rather, they are real, treatable medical illnesses in which certain maladaptive patterns of eating take on a life of their own. The main types of eating disorders are anorexia nervosa and bulimia nervosa. A third type, binge-eating disorder, has been suggested but has not yet been approved as a formal psychiatric diagnosis. Eating disorders frequently develop during adolescence or early adulthood, but some reports indicate their onset can occur during childhood or later in adulthood.

Eating disorders frequently co-occur with other psychiatric disorders such as depression, substance abuse, and anxiety disorders. In addition, people who suffer from eating disorders can experience a wide range of physical health complications, including serious heart conditions and kidney failure which may lead to death. Recognition of eating disorders as real and treatable diseases, therefore, is critically important.

Females are much more likely than males to develop an eating disorder. Only an estimated 5 to 15 percent of people with anorexia or bulimia and an estimated 35 percent of those with binge-eating disorder are male.

Anorexia Nervosa

An estimated 0.5 to 3.7 percent of females suffer from anorexia nervosa in their lifetime. Symptoms of anorexia nervosa include:

- Resistance to maintaining body weight at or above a minimally normal weight for age and height.
- Intense fear of gaining weight or becoming fat, even though underweight.
- Disturbance in the way in which one's body weight or shape is experienced, undue influence of body

A psychologist and two research analysts take a training seminar in clinical assessment of the genetics of anorexia nervosa. (AP Images)

weight or shape on self-evaluation, or denial of the seriousness of the current low body weight.

• Infrequent or absent menstrual periods (in females who have reached puberty).

People with this disorder see themselves as overweight even though they are dangerously thin. The process of eating becomes an obsession. Unusual eating habits develop, such as avoiding food and meals, picking out a few foods and eating these in small quantities, or carefully weighing and portioning food. People with anorexia may repeatedly check their body weight, and many engage in other techniques to control their weight, such as intense and compulsive exercise, or purging by means of vomiting and abuse of laxatives, enemas, and diuretics. Girls with anorexia often experience a delayed onset of their first menstrual period.

> **FAST FACT**
>
> So-called orthorexics are obsessed with food quality, rather than quantity, and strive for personal purity in their eating habits rather than a thin physique.

The course and outcome of anorexia nervosa vary across individuals: some fully recover after a single episode; some have a fluctuating pattern of weight gain and relapse; and others experience a chronically deteriorating course of illness over many years. The mortality rate among people with anorexia has been estimated at 0.56 percent per year, or approximately 5.6 percent per decade, which is about 12 times higher than the annual death rate due to all causes of death among females ages 15–24 in the general population. The most common causes of death are complications of the disorder, such as cardiac arrest or electrolyte imbalance, and suicide.

Bulimia Nervosa

An estimated 1.1 percent to 4.2 percent of females have bulimia nervosa in their lifetime. Symptoms of bulimia nervosa include:

• Recurrent episodes of binge eating, characterized by eating an excessive amount of food within a discrete period of time and by a sense of lack of control over eating during the episode.

• Recurrent inappropriate compensatory behavior in order to prevent weight gain, such as self-induced vomiting or misuse of laxatives, diuretics, enemas, or other medications (purging); fasting; or excessive exercise.

• The binge eating and inappropriate compensatory behaviors both occur, on average, at least twice a week for 3 months.

• Self-evaluation is unduly influenced by body shape and weight.

Because purging or other compensatory behavior follows the binge-eating episodes, people with bulimia usually weigh within the normal range for their age and height. However, like individuals with anorexia, they may fear gaining weight, desire to lose weight, and feel intensely dissatisfied with their bodies. People with bulimia often perform the behaviors in secrecy, feeling disgusted and ashamed when they binge, yet relieved once they purge.

Binge-Eating Disorder

Community surveys have estimated that between 2 percent and 5 percent of Americans experience binge-eating disorder in a 6-month period. Symptoms of binge-eating disorder include:

• Recurrent episodes of binge eating, characterized by eating an excessive amount of food within a discrete period of time and by a sense of lack of control over eating during the episode.

• The binge-eating episodes are associated with at least 3 of the following: eating much more rapidly than normal; eating until feeling uncomfortably full; eating large amounts of food when not feeling physically hungry; eating alone because of being embarrassed by how much one is eating; feeling disgusted with oneself, depressed, or very guilty after overeating.

- Marked distress about the binge-eating behavior.
- The binge eating occurs, on average, at least 2 days a week for 6 months.
- The binge eating is not associated with the regular use of inappropriate compensatory behaviors (e.g., purging, fasting, excessive exercise).

People with binge-eating disorder experience frequent episodes of out-of-control eating, with the same binge-eating symptoms as those with bulimia. The main difference is that individuals with binge-eating disorder do not purge their bodies of excess calories. Therefore, many with the disorder are overweight for their age and height. Feelings of self-disgust and shame associated with this illness can lead to bingeing again, creating a cycle of binge eating.

Treatment for Anorexia

Eating disorders can be treated and a healthy weight restored. The sooner these disorders are diagnosed and treated, the better the outcomes are likely to be. Because of their complexity, eating disorders require a comprehensive treatment plan involving medical care and monitoring, psychosocial interventions, nutritional counseling and, when appropriate, medication management. At the time of diagnosis, the clinician must determine whether the person is in immediate danger and requires hospitalization.

Treatment of anorexia calls for a specific program that involves three main phases: (1) restoring weight lost to severe dieting and purging; (2) treating psychological disturbances such as distortion of body image, low

Common Symptoms of Eating Disorders

Symptoms	Anorexia Nervosa*	Bulimia Nervosa*	Binge Eating Disorder
Excessive weight loss in relatively short period of time	✓		
Continuation of dieting although bone-thin	✓		
Dissatisfaction with appearance; belief that body is fat, even though severely underweight	✓		
Loss of monthly menstrual periods	✓	✓	
Unusual interest in food and development of strange eating rituals	✓	✓	
Eating in secret	✓	✓	✓
Obsession with exercise	✓	✓	
Serious depression	✓	✓	✓
Bingeing–consumption of large amounts of food		✓	✓
Vomiting or use of drugs to stimulate vomiting, bowel movements, and urination		✓	
Bingeing but no noticeable weight gain		✓	
Disappearance into bathroom for long periods of time to induce vomiting		✓	
Abuse of drugs or alcohol		✓	✓

*Some individuals suffer from anorexia and bulimia and have symptoms of both disorders.

Source: www.seekwellness.com.

self-esteem, and interpersonal conflicts; and (3) achieving long-term remission and rehabilitation, or full recovery.

Early diagnosis and treatment increases the treatment success rate. Use of psychotropic medication in people with anorexia should be considered *only* after weight gain has been established. Certain selective serotonin reuptake inhibitors (SSRIs) have been shown to be helpful for weight maintenance and for resolving mood and anxiety symptoms associated with anorexia.

The acute management of severe weight loss is usually provided in an inpatient hospital setting, where feeding plans address the person's medical and nutritional needs. In some cases, intravenous feeding is recommended. Once malnutrition has been corrected and weight gain has begun, psychotherapy (often cognitive-behavioral or interpersonal psychotherapy) can help people with anorexia overcome low self-esteem and address distorted thought and behavior patterns. Families are sometimes included in the therapeutic process.

Treatment for Bulimia

The primary goal of treatment for bulimia is to reduce or eliminate binge eating and purging behavior. To this end, nutritional rehabilitation, psychosocial intervention, and medication management strategies are often employed. Establishment of a pattern of regular, non-binge meals, improvement of attitudes related to the eating disorder, encouragement of healthy but not excessive exercise, and resolution of co-occurring conditions such as mood or anxiety disorders are among the specific aims of these strategies.

Individual psychotherapy (especially cognitive-behavioral or interpersonal psychotherapy), group psychotherapy that uses a cognitive-behavioral approach, and family or marital therapy have been reported to be effective. Psychotropic medications, primarily antidepressants such as . . . SSRIs, have been found helpful for people with bulimia, particularly those with significant symptoms of depression or anxiety, or those who have not responded adequately to psychosocial treatment alone. These medications also may help prevent relapse.

The treatment goals and strategies for binge-eating disorder are similar to those for bulimia, and studies are currently evaluating the effectiveness of various interventions.

Eating Disorders Are a Serious Matter

Andrea Faiad

In the following article Andrea Faiad explains that roughly 10 million girls and women and about 1 million boys and men suffer from eating disorders. The causes of eating disorders are varied, contends Faiad, and include family history, metabolism, personality, and involvement in certain sports that require a specific body type. If left untreated, the disease can lead to death from lack of food, dehydration, and organ failure. The author concludes that treatment, such as that provided by the Renfrew Center, gives sufferers confidence in themselves so they can beat their illness. Andrea Faiad is a lifestyle reporter for the *Post-Bulletin* in Rochester, Minnesota, and a freelance writer for *Teen People* magazine.

To people who don't know his story, Matthew Cornwall of Quincy, Ill., is like most 11-year-old boys. He likes computers, riding his bike, and play-

SOURCE: Andrea Faiad, "To Your Mind Dying To Be Thin," *Current Health* 1, vol. 30, November 2006, pp. 20–23. Special permission granted by Weekly Reader, published and copyrighted by Weekly Reader Corporation. All rights reserved.

ing with LEGO blocks. He likes his pet hermit crabs and his cat. But unlike most kids his age, he nearly starved himself to death.

When Matthew was 9 years old, he started reading food labels and refusing to eat almost anything with fat in it. Matthew was already small for his age, but, he says, "I wanted to be the skinniest in the class." A few months later, Matthew was so sick that his parents drove him through the night to an eating disorder treatment program in Omaha, Neb. "I was scared," Matthew remembers. "They believed I wasn't going to make it. I was afraid I was going to die."

About 1 million males and 10 million females in the United States are reported to have eating disorders. Of

Who Is at Risk?

These are signs of an eating disorder. Having one or more symptoms is a reason to get help:

1. Insisting on weighing less than the normal weight for height, age, and body type.

2. Being obsessed with counting calories.

3. Needing to weigh yourself several times a day.

4. Being obsessed with how certain body parts look (such as the legs, bottom, or stomach).

5. Eating large amounts of food and then trying to rid the body of it.

6. Having food rituals, such as taking tiny bites, skipping food groups, or rearranging food on the plate.

7. Avoiding meals or only wanting to eat alone.

8. Viewing yourself as fat no matter what your size.

Source: National Eating Disorders Association.

those people, about 660,000 end up dying from their illnesses.

What Are Eating Disorders?

Eating disorders are illnesses that cause a person to have harmful eating habits. Anorexia nervosa and bulimia are the two most common types of eating disorders.

Anorexia is an illness in which a person purposely starves herself or himself. The person has an intense fear of gaining weight or becoming fat, even if she or he is underweight.

Bulimia is an illness in which a person repeatedly overeats and purges—for example, vomits (throws up)

People with eating disorders are prone to changes in personality, character, and physical well- being. (AP Images)

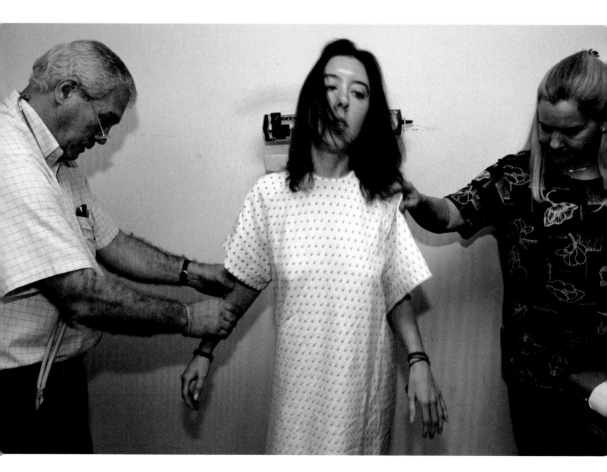

on purpose or exercises more than is healthy to burn off the extra calories.

What Triggers an Eating Disorder?

Anyone can develop an eating disorder. Anorexia and bulimia have been found in every race, culture, and age-group throughout the world. In fact, anorexia is the third-most-common ongoing illness among young teens.

Experts say a combination of factors causes a person to develop an eating disorder. The causes include family history (like a parent with an eating disorder), metabolism (how fast the body burns calories), personality (such as how well a teen handles problems), and family issues. Playing a sport that puts pressure on the athlete to be a certain weight and admiring dangerously thin celebrities also may play a role. Using alcohol or drugs, feeling depressed, or having relationship troubles can also put a person at risk.

In Matthew's case, his mom thinks that a recent move, his sister's going off to college, and several TV programs talking about obesity came together to cause Matthew's anorexia.

> **FAST FACT**
>
> As recently as the 1980s, people still did not recognize names for or understand eating disorders.

Spotting an Eating Disorder

Just looking at someone's weight doesn't necessarily show whether he or she has an eating disorder. For example, many people who have bulimia are of normal weight or slightly above-normal weight, according to Doug Bunnell, a psychologist with the Renfrew Center Foundation for Eating Disorders. The Renfrew Center specializes in treating anorexia, bulimia, and other eating disorders. "You have to look at what they're doing with food and what their thoughts and feelings are," Bunnell says. "My greatest concern is that people think these are relatively mild disorders,"

Bunnell says. "[Teens] think they're really not at risk for anything serious."

Eating Disorders Are Serious

The reality is that anorexia is the number one cause of death among girls ages 15 to 24. That's according to the Renfrew Center.

Eating disorders can cause dangerous physical problems, including malnutrition (a lack of enough healthy food) and dehydration (a lack of fluids). Eating disorders can also cause serious damage to the stomach, heart, kidneys, liver, gums, teeth, and esophagus (which moves food to your stomach). Many people with eating disorders also lose muscle and feel weak. Their heart muscle can break down and become damaged over time. This can result in an increased risk of the heart's stopping.

Eating disorders also can cause emotional problems, such as mood swings and hurt relationships with family and friends.

Changes in Personality Accompany Eating Disorders

"It's hard for the people around you because they really have to walk on eggshells," says Jen S., 16, of Boca Raton, Fla. She began struggling with anorexia at age 13. "I was very defensive. I wasn't the person they'd had as a sister or daughter before," she says.

Before she developed anorexia, Jen says, she was a fun, carefree person and, in general, happy. "But with my eating disorder, my personality fell away, and I became a ridiculous perfectionist," she says. "I also began to lie and manipulate . . . so people wouldn't know how little I truly ate."

In addition to the changes in her personality and character, she suffered physically; for example, she had severe acid reflux (a painful burning in the chest and throat) from a lack of food in her stomach. In addition, her hair fell out in clumps, tiny hairs grew all over her

Pressure to "look perfect for the camera" can be a major factor in eating disorders among celebrities. (AP Images)

body, and her nails became very brittle and sometimes fell off.

"Those effects scare me every day," Jen says. "How much did I permanently damage my whole body?" She remembers dangerously limiting her food in eighth grade. Her weight fell dramatically. Finally, in ninth grade, she faced the fact that she had to either get help or risk dying. At half her pre-anorexia weight, she checked in to the Renfrew Center. In therapy, she came to understand that her father's death might have triggered her eating disorder. (He died of cancer when she was 7.)

"You look for something else to get your mind off [your problems], so you start controlling things. For me, my controlling was my schoolwork and my food," Jen says.

Recovery Is Possible

Taking care of body image or eating problems in their beginning stages can be difficult. But that recognition gives the best chance for working through the issues and becoming healthy again. To recover, Jen says, she had to change the way she thinks. "I used to be very hard on myself and very competitive and never felt like I was good enough," Jen says. She continues to go to therapy. "I dealt with so much in treatment and learned so much about myself—probably the biggest thing was to be proud of myself."

Treatments for Eating Disorders Must Address Physical and Psychological Issues

HealthyPlace.com

The following article advises people with eating disorders to seek medical and psychological help as soon as possible. The longer an eating disorder persists, the more damage it causes to the body and the more long-term treatment will be required. General treatment typically involves a variety of experts, such as an internist, a nutritionist, a psychotherapist, and a psychopharmacologist, according to the Web site. Specifically, people suffering from anorexia usually require a combination of hospitalization, an inpatient psychiatric program that includes family therapy, pharmaceuticals, and self-management that includes maintaining an ideal weight and functioning independently in daily activities. People with bulimia may not require hospitalization but can benefit from outpatient treatment, long-term psychotherapy to develop and improve self-control, and antidepressants. Compulsive overeaters should receive treatment for both symptoms of depression and the compulsive habit of overeating. Their treatment should also include lifestyle modification, diet, and exercise. HealthyPlace.com is an online eating disorders community providing mental health information, support, and the opportunity to share experiences helpful to others.

SOURCE: "Eating Disorders Treatment for Anorexia, Bulimia," HealthyPlace.com.

Eating disorders are most successfully treated when diagnosed early. Unfortunately, even when family members confront the ill person about his or her behavior, or physicians make a diagnosis, individuals with eating disorders may deny that they have a problem. Thus, people with anorexia may not receive medical or psychological attention until they have already become dangerously thin and malnourished. People with bulimia are often normal weight and are able to hide their illness from others for years. Eating disorders in males may be overlooked because anorexia and bulimia are relatively rare in boys and men. Consequently, getting—and keeping—people with these disorders into treatment can be extremely difficult.

Seek Treatment as Soon as Possible

In any case, it cannot be overemphasized how important treatment is—the sooner, the better. The longer abnormal eating behaviors persist, the more difficult it is to overcome the disorder and its effects on the body. In some cases, long-term treatment may be required. Families and friends offering support and encouragement can play an important role in the success of the treatment program.

Unrealistic Expectations

	Average Woman	Barbie Doll	Store Mannequin
Height	5'4"	6'0"	6'0"
Weight	145 lbs	101 lbs	Not available
Dress size	11 – 14	4	6
Bust	36 – 37'	39'	34'
Waist	29 – 31'	19'	23'
Hips	40 – 42'	33'	34'

Source: Anorexia and Related Eating Disorders Inc., www.anred.com/stats.html.

If an eating disorder is suspected, particularly if it involves weight loss, the first step is a complete physical examination to rule out any other illnesses. Once an eating disorder is diagnosed, the clinician must determine whether the patient is in immediate medical danger and requires hospitalization. While most patients can be treated as outpatients, some need hospital care.

Conditions warranting hospitalization include excessive and rapid weight loss, serious metabolic disturbances, clinical depression or risk of suicide, severe binge eating and purging, or psychosis.

Psychotherapy Treats Underlying Emotional Issues

The complex interaction of emotional and physiological problems in eating disorders calls for a comprehensive treatment plan, involving a variety of experts and approaches. Ideally, the treatment team includes an internist, a nutritionist, an individual psychotherapist, and a psychopharmacologist—someone who is knowledgeable about psychoactive medications useful in treating these disorders.

To help those with eating disorders deal with their illness and underlying emotional issues, some form of psychotherapy is usually needed. A psychiatrist, psychologist, or other mental health professional meets with the patient individually and provides ongoing emotional support, while the patient begins to understand and cope with the illness. Group therapy, in which people share their experiences with others who have similar problems, has been especially effective for individuals with bulimia.

Use of individual psychotherapy, family therapy, and cognitive-behavioral therapy—a form of psychotherapy that teaches patients how to change abnormal thoughts and behavior—is often the most productive. Cognitive-behavior therapists focus on changing eating behaviors usually by rewarding or modeling wanted behavior.

These therapists also help patients work to change the distorted and rigid thinking patterns associated with eating disorders.

Antidepressant Medications May Help

National Institute of Mental Health–supported scientists have examined the effectiveness of combining psychotherapy and medications. In a recent study of bulimia, researchers found that both intensive group therapy and antidepressant medications, combined or alone, benefited patients. In another study of bulimia, the combined use of cognitive-behavioral therapy and antidepressant medications was most beneficial. The combination treatment was particularly effective in preventing relapse once medications were discontinued. For patients with binge eating disorder, cognitive-behavioral therapy and antidepressant medications may also prove to be useful.

Antidepressant medications commonly used to treat bulimia include desipramine, imipramine, and fluoxetine. For anorexia, preliminary evidence shows that some antidepressant medications may be effective when combined with other forms of treatment. Fluoxetine has also been useful in treating some patients with binge eating disorder. These antidepressants may also treat any co-occurring depression.

The efforts of mental health professionals need to be combined with those of other health professionals to obtain the best treatment. Physicians treat any medical complications, and nutritionists advise on diet and eating regimens. The challenge of treating eating disorders is made more difficult by the metabolic changes associated with them. Just to maintain a stable weight, individuals with anorexia may actually have to consume more calories than someone of similar weight and age without an eating disorder.

This information is important for patients and the clinicians who treat them. Consuming calories is exactly what the person with anorexia wishes to avoid, yet must do to regain the weight necessary for recovery. In contrast, some normal weight people with bulimia may gain excess weight if they consume the number of calories required to maintain normal weight in others of similar size and age.

Treatment for Anorexia

The course of anorexia nervosa varies greatly among patients, ranging from spontaneous recovery without treatment, to recovery after a variety of treatments; to a fluctuating course of weight gain followed by relapse; or, rarely, to a gradually deteriorating course resulting in death caused by complications of starvation.

By the time a person with anorexia nervosa comes to medical attention, the disorder usually has progressed to a considerable degree, and weight loss has become apparent. Often, amenorrhea (ending of monthly periods) is the first manifestation of the disorder to come to the attention of the physician, as it often appears before weight loss is noticeable. From 30 to 50 percent of anorexia nervosa patients also have the symptoms of bulimia nervosa.

In general, the prognosis for anorexia nervosa is not favorable. While a patient may return to his or her normal weight, moderate to severe preoccupation with food and body weight often continues, social relationships are frequently impaired, and many patients are clinically depressed. Studies have shown a range of mortality rates from 5 to 18 percent, although the higher rates almost certainly occur in persons with associated disorders (e.g., depression, OCD, or substance abuse). . . .

Hospitalization

A successful eating disorder treatment program should address both the physical and psychological aspects of

FAST FACT

Anorexic patients attest to spending 70 to 85 percent of each day thinking about food, what to eat, what to feed others, when to binge, and when to purge.

the eating disorder. The patient, who is often initially reluctant, must be a willing participant in the treatment plan to maintain long-term positive outcomes. Hospitalization, psychotherapy and pharmacotherapy are all viable treatment options.

The first consideration in the treatment of anorexia nervosa is to restore the patient's nutritional state, since dehydration, starvation and electrolyte imbalances can lead to serious health problems and, in some cases, death. According to *The New Harvard Guide to Psychiatry* (Nicholi, ed. 1988), suggested criteria for hospitalization include:

- weight loss of greater than 30 percent over three months
- severe metabolic disturbance
- severe depression or suicide risk
- severe binging and purging
- failure to maintain outpatient weight contract
- complex differential diagnosis
- psychosis
- family crisis
- need for confrontation of individual and family denial, and initiation of individual and family therapy and pharmcotherapy

Inpatient psychiatric programs for anorexia nervosa patients generally use a combination of behavioral therapy, individual psychotherapy, family education and therapy, and, in some cases, psychotropic medications.

Patients often resist admission and, for the first several weeks of eating disorder treatment, will make dramatic pleas for the family's support to obtain release from the hospital program. In addition, the vast majority of patients with anorexia nervosa require continued intervention after discharge from the hospital.

Psychotherapy and Pharmacotherapy

Many clinicians prefer cognitive-behavioral approaches to monitor weight gain and maintenance and to address eating behaviors. Cognitive or interpersonal strategies also have been recommended to explore other issues related to the disorder, such as depression. Family therapy has been used to examine interactions among family members, since unresolved conflict within the family is often implicated in the illness.

While clinical studies have not yet identified a medication that improves the core symptoms of anorexia nervosa, several medications have demonstrated benefit. Some studies support the use of Periactin® (cyproheptadine), which has both antihistaminic and antiserotonergic properties, in the restricting type (no binge eating or purging behavior) of anorexia. Elavil® (amitriptyline) also has been reported to have some benefit in anorexia patients.

In patients with coexisting depressive disorders, other antidepressants have shown little benefit. In addition, the use of tricyclic drugs in low-weight, depressed patients can be risky, since these patients may be vulnerable to hypotension, cardiac arrhythmia and dehydration.

Some evidence indicates that electroconvulsive therapy (ECT) is also beneficial in certain cases of anorexia nervosa with major depressive disorder.

Self-Management

To make the fullest possible recovery, a person with anorexia must:

1. Participate actively in the treatment plan.

2. Complete the inpatient program when necessary.

3. Maintain weight independently within 5 pounds of assigned target weight.

4. Function independently in activities of daily living.

5. Regularly attend individual, group and/or family psychotherapy.

6. Regularly visit your internist to safeguard your physical health.

7. Demonstrate effective coping skills.

8. Ask for assistance when needed.

9. Be honest with your therapist and internist. No withholding of information.

Treatment of Bulimia

Little is known about the long-term course of bulimia nervosa, and the short-term outcome is variable. However, it seems to have a better prognosis than anorexia nervosa. In the short run, bulimia patients who are treated report more than 50 percent improvement in binging and purging; among outpatients, improvement seems to last more than five years. The patients, however, are not symptom-free during periods of improvement, as bulimia is a chronic disorder that waxes and wanes.

Generally, bulimia nervosa patients are not as secretive about their symptoms as are patients with anorexia, and are typically more receptive to treatment. Treatment of bulimia may consist of individual psychotherapy, group therapy, family therapy and/or pharmacotherapy. Since bulimia nervosa often coexists with mood disorders, anxiety disorders and personality disorders, the doctor should factor these considerations into the patient's treatment plan.

Hospitalization

Most patients with uncomplicated bulimia nervosa do not require hospitalization. Because patients with bulimia are not as secretive about their symptoms as anorexia patients, outpatient treatment is usually sufficient. However, when eating binges are extreme, if patients exhibit other psychiatric symptoms such as suicidal ideation and substance abuse, or if purging is so severe it causes electrolyte and metabolic disturbances, hospitalization may be warranted. As symptoms are brought under control and both eating behaviors and weight are stabilized, control is gradually and slowly returned to the patient. At all levels of care, the treatment usually involves high levels of structure and a behavioral treatment plan based on the patient's weight and eating behaviors. Long-term psychotherapy and medical follow-up with an internist are usually necessary.

Psychotherapy and Pharmacotherapy

The goal of therapy is to help patients develop or improve self-control and judgment. Cognitive-behavioral psychotherapy has been shown to be useful in addressing the specific behaviors that lead to binging episodes. However, many patients have coexisting disorders (i.e., mood disorders and substance-related disorders) that go beyond the behavior surrounding binge eating. Therefore, additional psychotherapeutic approaches (such as psychodynamic, interpersonal and family therapies) can be useful.

Group therapy is also an appropriate treatment for patients with bulimia. Three major models of outpatient group therapy for bulimics have been developed: psychodynamically oriented psychotherapy, cognitive-behavioral therapy and self-help (support group) therapy (Nicholi, ed. *The New Harvard Guide to Psychiatry*, 1988).

Antidepressants have been successfully used in patients who are not responsive to psychotherapy alone. (The FDA recently approved Prozac® for the treatment of bulimia nervosa.) Tofranil® (imipramine), Norpramin® (desipramine), Desyrel® (trazodone), selective serotonin reuptake inhibitors (SSRIs) and monoamine oxidase inhibitors (MAOIs) have all suggested efficacy in small trials.

Self-Management

To make the fullest possible recovery, a person with bulimia must:

1. Participate actively in the treatment plan.
2. Complete the inpatient program when necessary.
3. Maintain weight independently within 5 pounds of assigned target weight.
4. Function independently in activities of daily living.
5. Regularly attend individual, group and/or family psychotherapy.
6. Regularly visit your internist to safeguard your physical health.
7. Demonstrate effective coping skills.
8. Ask for assistance when needed.
9. Be honest with your therapist and internist. No withholding of information.

Treatment for Compulsive Overeating

Treatment programs that address only the depression, will not be successful in breaking the cycle of compulsive overeating. The compulsive overeater needs treatment for both the clinical symptoms of depression, and the behavior of compulsive eating, to successfully end this vicious cycle.

The most effective weight loss programs are comprehensive: they combine diet, behavior modification (life-style change), nutritional education, exercise, medication (where appropriate) and long-term maintenance support.

As for pharmacologic treatment, compulsive overeaters are primarily treated with antidepressants. Psychological treatment, particularly cognitive/behavioral therapy and interpersonal therapy, is as effective as antidepressants in the short-term. However, in the long-term, psychological treatment is more effective.

Recovering from compulsive overeating and losing weight are extremely difficult processes and require long-term changes with professional guidance to help you learn new eating habits [to] maintain long-term weight loss.

Weight Control Techniques

1. Keep a food diary for a week to become aware of your eating habits.
2. Eat all meals and snacks in one location.
3. Sit down when eating.
4. Avoid other activities while eating.
5. Eat slowly.
6. Use a smaller plate or bowl.
7. Try to avoid seconds. If you must, choose a salad or vegetable.
8. Stay away from the kitchen except for meals.
9. Don't keep problem foods around.
10. Grocery shop at a time when you're not hungry.
11. Store food out of sight.
12. Find responses other than eating to feelings like boredom, sadness, anxiety, loneliness, frustration and anger.
13. Find other ways to reward yourself besides eating.
14. Exercise regularly.
15. Weigh yourself no more often than once a week.
16. Set goals to change eating behaviors. Make small changes and be patient with yourself. Changing habits takes time and work.

More Men Are Diagnosed with Eating Disorders

Ovetta Wiggins

Although girls and women are the majority of those afflicted with eating disorders, the incidence of boys and men becoming preoccupied with looking fat is increasing, claims Ovetta Wiggins in the following article. About one in ten people who suffer from an eating disorder is male. In the last five to ten years, more men have succumbed to society's obsession with body image and with the nearly impossible-to-attain proportions of the models on the covers of glossy fitness magazines. Wiggins previews a University of Maryland program to educate male students on self-esteem and proper eating habits as a proactive measure against male eating disorders. Ovetta Wiggins is a metro reporter for the *Washington Post*.

Jane Jakubczak, dietitian at the University Health Center at the University of Maryland at College Park, gets the same query from students that she did when she took the job five years ago.

SOURCE: Ovetta Wiggins, "More Men Struggling With Eating Issues, Doctors Say," *The Washington Post*, September 30, 2004, p. SM05. Copyright © 2004, The Washington Post. Reprinted with permission.

"What can I eat to get the fat off my body?"

What has changed, Jakubczak said, is that male students are posing the questions. With increasing frequency, she said, young men are starving themselves in pursuit of bodies that fulfill a magazine ideal.

"I have students asking, what can I eat to get rid of love handles? And they pinch, and there's nothing there," Jakubczak said.

Increase in Males with ED Is Recent

Three years ago, Jakubczak saw about four male students during the school year who were asking for help to lose weight. These days, she said, she sees at least one a week.

In addition to asking about how to look like someone on the cover of a fitness magazine, male students are doing extreme dieting, exercising compulsively, using food supplements or combining all three, Jakubczak said.

Randi Wortman, a clinical psychologist who works with men and women with eating disorders at her Bethesda, Md., office, said the increase in male eating disorders is only about five to 10 years old.

"For women it comes from the Twiggy [a very thin British model of the late 1960s] generation," Wortman said. "Since the fitness craze with the glossy health magazines, men have become part of society's overinflated vision of what is the ideal body type."

Jakubczak said some of her male students have taken all of the fat out of their diets in an attempt to "get the abs of the guy on the *Men's Health* cover."

"They are coming in desperate," she said. "They come in to see me for what are distorted eating habits and distorted body images."

One in Ten People with an ED Is Male

Signs of an eating disorder include excessive dieting and fasting, a fear of becoming fat or gaining weight, and a preoccupation with food and low sense of self-worth.

Health officials say the experience at the University Health Center mirrors what is happening nationwide.

One of every 10 people with an eating disorder who comes to the attention of mental health professionals is male, according to the National Eating Disorders Association.

Julie Parsons, a clinical social worker and coordinator of the eating disorder program at the University Health Center, said eating disorders remain more prevalent among women than men, but the numbers of men "who are aware they are bothered by their relationship with food" have increased.

Girls are not the only ones who have social pressure put on them to be thin. (© Heiko Wolfraum/dpa/CORBIS)

Parsons said men are experiencing what women have dealt with for years. They are bombarded with magazine versions of body images that are almost unrealistic.

[In 2003] the university's Center for Health and Well-being held a weeklong program to educate male students about the differences between improving body image and pursuing such changes obsessively.

. . . The center will [also] host a program to discuss dieting and body shape and size. The program targets men, but organizers did not focus on eating disorders because they fear many men would feel too embarrassed to come.

"The hard part is to get the dialogue open without turning people away," Jakubczak said. "It's a slow process making men aware of the issue."

> **FAST FACT**
>
> In a 2003 survey at the University of Maryland at College Park, one in two male students indicated that he was dieting, eating special foods, or taking supplements to lose weight.

Binge Eating Is Now the Most Common Eating Disorder

Nicholas Bakalar

A survey by Harvard researchers concluded that binge eating is a more common eating disorder than anorexia and bulimia, estimated to affect about 2.8 percent of the general population. Binge eating is described as eating an inordinately large amount of food in a two-hour period at least twice a week for six months. People who binge eat feel that they have no control over their eating habits and have been found to suffer from other psychiatric illnesses as well, such as depression, phobias, and substance abuse. If binge eating is recognized as a legitimate psychiatric disorder, patients will be able to receive appropriate treatment. Nicholas Bakalar, PhD, is a writer for the *New York Times* and the author of more than ten books, including *AIDS* and *People with Severe Mental Illness*.

Binge eating is not yet officially classified as a psychiatric disorder. But it may be more common than the two eating disorders now recognized, anorexia nervosa and bulimia.

SOURCE: Nicholas Bakalar, "Survey Puts New Focus on Binge Eating as a Diagnosis," *The New York Times*, February 13, 2007, p. F5. Copyright © 2007 by The New York Times Company. Reprinted with permission.

The first nationally representative study of eating disorders in the United States, a nationwide survey of more than 2,900 men and women, was published by Harvard researchers in the Feb. 1 issue of the journal *Biological Psychiatry*. It found a prevalence in the general population of 0.6 percent for anorexia, 1 percent for bulimia and 2.8 percent for binge-eating disorder.

Lifetime rates of the disorders, the researchers found, are higher in younger age groups, suggesting that the problem is increasingly common. Eating disorders are about twice as common among women as men, the study reports.

Binge Eating Recognized as a Disorder

Experts not involved in the study called it significant. "This is probably the best study yet conducted of the frequencies of eating disorders in American households," said Dr. B. Timothy Walsh, director of the eating disorders research unit of the New York State Psychiatric Institute at Columbia University Medical Center.

"It confirms that anorexia nervosa and bulimia are uncommon but serious illnesses, especially among women," Dr. Walsh said. "It also finds that many more individuals, especially those with significant obesity, are troubled by binge eating, and underscores the need to better understand this problem."

The survey, partly financed by two pharmaceutical companies, was carried out from 2001 to 2003 among adults 18 and older, and the diagnoses were established using face-to-face interviews.

While all three eating disorders appear in the American Psychiatric Association's diagnostic bible, the *Diagnostic and Statistical Manual of Mental Disorders, or D.S.M.-IV*, binge eating disorder is not considered a definitive diagnosis like anorexia and bulimia. Rather, it is one of a number of categories requiring further study.

A "Medicalized" Diagnosis or Just Human Behavior?

Some suspect that establishing binge eating disorder as a psychiatric diagnosis is merely an attempt by psychiatrists or drug companies to "medicalize" what would otherwise be considered simply ordinary, if unfortunate, human behavior. Cynthia M. Bulik, director of the eat-

Buffets can be a binge eater's nightmare.
(AP Images)

ing disorders program at the University of North Carolina, Chapel Hill, does not see it this way.

"It's patients who want this in the D.S.M. so they can get treatment," Dr. Bulik said. "I've gotten e-mails from people saying, 'Thanks for putting a name on this binge-eating disorder.'

"The disorder has no diagnostic label that will get them insurance payments," she continued. "They have a nasty syndrome with serious health implications, knowing that there is evidence-based treatment available and not being able to get it because it's not officially recognized as a diagnosis."

A Feeling That You Can't Stop Eating

The diagnosis of binge eating disorder requires that a person eat an excessively large amount of food in a two-hour period at least twice a week for six months, feel a lack of control over the episodes, and experience marked distress regarding the practice.

Marlene B. Schwartz, the director of research and school programs at the Rudd Center for Food Policy and Obesity at Yale, who had no role in the study, said binge-eating disorders were "not a matter of just eating too much every now and then."

"The diagnosis requires the feeling that you can't stop," Dr. Schwartz said. "And it's that loss of control that makes it a psychiatric disorder different from someone just overindulging every now and then."

Dr. James I. Hudson, the lead author of the new study, said binge eating was associated with obesity, particularly severe obesity. "This brings in a lot of medical consequences and suggests it's a major health problem," he said. "This information will help us make decisions on public health policy." Dr. Hudson is director of the psychiatric epidemiology research program at McLean

> ## FAST FACT
>
> Binge-eating disorder was not named until 1992, finally allowing individuals affected to seek clinical help.

Hospital in Belmont, Mass., and a professor of psychiatry at Harvard.

Eating Disorders Accompanied by Other Psychiatric Illnesses

A diagnosis of anorexia requires a refusal to maintain at least 85 percent of normal weight and a distinctly distorted view of one's weight or body shape. Bulimia is characterized by recurrent episodes of binge eating at least twice a week for three months and then compensating for the behavior, usually by self-induced vomiting or abuse of laxatives and other medicines.

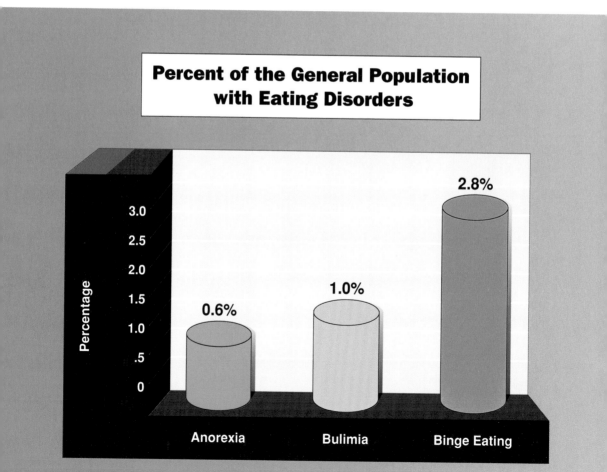

Percent of the General Population with Eating Disorders

Anorexia 0.6%
Bulimia 1.0%
Binge Eating 2.8%

Source: Nicholas Bakalar, "Survey Puts New Focus on Binge Eating as a Diagnosis," *The New York Times*, February 13, 2007, p. F5.

Eating disorders, the researchers found, are commonly accompanied by other psychiatric illnesses. In the survey, more than half of the people with bulimia had major depression, 50 percent had phobias and more than one-third had a substance abuse disorder. Over all, more than 94 percent of people with bulimia, 56 percent of those with anorexia and 79 percent of those with binge-eating disorder had at least one other psychiatric diagnosis.

Dr. Hudson said the most significant limitation of the study was its basis on self-reports, explaining that people tend to underreport their problems with eating disorders. So the true prevalence, he said, is probably higher than reported.

"Obesity is an endpoint, and there are many pathways in," Dr. Bulik said. "One of the things I look for is modifiable behavioral factors. This study shows now that binge eating disorder is relatively prevalent. For a certain percentage of the population, this is a modifiable behavior."

CHAPTER 2

The Controversial Side of Eating Disorders

Mental Illness Contributes to Eating Disorders

Elena Rozwadowski

In the following article Elena Rozwadowski reports how various mental illnesses and eating disorders run hand in hand. Depression and anxiety often accompany eating disorders, and medication can alleviate the helplessness and anxiousness that young women with eating disorders suffer, explains Rozwadowski. Post-traumatic stress, such as that following sexual abuse, can trigger a response in women who want to take control of their bodies; unfortunately that means starving themselves or bingeing and purging. Rozwadowski adds that college women are susceptible to developing eating disorders because they want to fit in with their peers. Treatment involves support from family and friends to address the mental health issues that lead to eating disorders. Elena Rozwadowski writes for the *Minnesota Daily*, the newspaper of the University of Minnesota, and the *Star Tribune* in Minneapolis, Minnesota.

Photo on facing page. Randall Terry speaks about the case of Terry Schiavo outside the Pinellas County courthouse. The case created much publicity for the problem of eating disorders. **(AP Images)**

W hile in high school, Megan Kosse was a straight-A student with a flair for debate.----- But she never felt like that was good enough.

"I would tell my mom that whatever I did was mediocre," said Megan, an anthropology and Spanish junior. "I felt like trying to compensate." She started taking diet pills and restricting her food to try to gain control of her body and her mind. Sometimes she would binge eat to make herself better.

When Megan got to the University of Minnesota, the binge eating increased.

"I remember hitting all the milestones—5, 10, 15 pounds heavier," she said.

At one point, she started cutting her stomach to deal with the depression and anxiety.

"It took the focus off. It was the only thing that could make my mind stop," she said. "That's all I wanted to do in the first place." In the world of eating disorders, Megan's situation is not unusual.

Mental Health Problems Accompany Eating Disorders

Diann Ackard, a private-practice psychologist in Golden Valley who specializes in eating disorders, said the disorders can serve as a distraction from other mental health problems.

"Eating disorders can help numb intense feelings," Ackard said. "It's like an 'anesthesia' for emotions." With help from her mom, Megan made an appointment at the Service for Teenagers at Risk Clinic for Family Health in the McNamara Alumni Center, where she was given medication for her depression and anxiety.

"I always thought binge eating wasn't a big deal; it was just my form of a diet," Megan said. "But you can die from it." Depression and anxiety are two of the more common mental health problems that accompany eating disorders.

In fact, 50 percent to 75 percent of patients with anorexia or bulimia have problems with depression, according to the American Psychiatric Association.

Depression Can Cause Eating Disorders

Depression can often cause eating problems, said Candice Price, a clinical social worker at Boynton Health Service.

"When you see someone for depression, they may have an issue with food, meaning they may have lost weight because they're not eating because they're depressed," she said. "There's overlap, but the eating disorder is not necessarily a given." Other internal and external factors can trigger the disorders, Ackard said.

"There are genetic components involved and there are also environmental components involved," she said. "There

Major Diagnostic Classes of Mental Disorders

Disorders usually first diagnosed in infancy, childhood, or adolescence

Delirium, dementia, and amnesic and other cognitive disorders

Mental disorders due to a general medical condition

Substance-related disorders

Schizophrenia and other psychotic disorders

Mood disorders

Anxiety disorders

Somatoform disorders

Factitious disorders

Dissociative disorders

Sexual and gender identity disorders

Eating disorders

Sleep disorders

Impulse-control disorders

Adjustment disorders

Personality disorders

Source: www.surgeongeneral.gov/library/mentalhealth/chapter2/sec2.html.

is a genetic predisposition for many individuals who have eating disorders, but it seems the environment has to play a role in triggering those genes to activate." Other common issues include obsessive compulsive disorder, bipolar disorder and different personality disorders that affect a person's emotional reactions to a situation.

Trauma and Sexual Abuse

Post-traumatic stress disorder is also a common trigger for eating disorders, especially when sexual abuse is involved.

Up to 50 percent of anorexia and bulimia nervosa patients have reported sexual abuse in their past, according to American Psychiatric Association statistics.

Ackard described trauma as a "nonspecific risk factor" with eating disorders, which means trauma can make a person susceptible to many different mental health issues.

> **FAST FACT**
>
> The tendency toward anxiety and depression indicates the possible onset of eating disorders.

"In cases of violence to the body, the body is the site where the trauma occurred," she said. In these cases, she said, the person may want to change their body in order to erase the trauma.

"In terms of sexual abuse in women, a woman may want to lose weight in order to revert back to what they see as the safety of a younger time," she said.

College Environment

The college environment can also trigger eating disorders from both an environmental and developmental standpoint.

According to the American Psychiatric Association, eating disorders are the third most common chronic illness to affect college women, after obesity and asthma, respectively.

Everything from the infamous "freshman 15" to the college lifestyle can trigger an eating disorder, said Carol

Support groups can help with the mental illnesses related to eating disorders. **(AP Images)**

Tappen, director of operations for the St. Louis Park–based Eating Disorders Institute.

Sometimes the pressure to fit in can be a big factor in eating disorders in the college environment.

"There's the example of the young woman who's always been a little heavy who gets to college and everyone around her is bone-thin," Tappen said. "There may be bingeing and purging in the dorms or the sorority houses and that young woman gets caught up in it because she wants to belong." Because mental health issues and eating disorders are so intertwined, it is often difficult to treat one before the other, Tappen said.

Support from Family and Friends

"Symptom interruption is huge," she said, and one of the first goals in most treatment programs is developing a normal eating pattern. "The key is to interrupt the cycle while the patient is clinically contained," Tappen said.

Support from family and friends can be key to successful treatment, she said.

"Families have to be involved," Tappen said, because a family member might need education and support when one of them has an eating disorder.

"We have to make sure nobody's blaming themselves," she said.

Tappen said it is often helpful for patients to pick up the phone and talk to a family member who "gets it." "I believe you always need two or three people that you can talk to who have said you can call them morning, noon or night," she said.

University psychiatry professor Scott Crow said it's often easier to treat the eating problems first because they bring so many problems with them, especially in anorexia patients.

"Starvation really tends to impact thinking," he said.

The mental health problems can often be the most problematic parts of treatment, Crow said.

"Unless you can reverse the anorexia at least a little bit, it can be almost impossible to treat the other problems," he said.

One of the biggest problems with treatment is each patient's differing needs.

"The diagnostic criteria don't work very well," Crow said.

Many people will be diagnosed as anorexic and a few months later, show symptoms of bulimia, he said.

"The reason you group people together is to better make predictions," Crow said. "That's something we can't do with as much confidence when it comes to eating disorders." To better understand eating disorders, the University psychiatry department is conducting a study on anorexia.

Mental Health Study

The study, funded by the National Institute of Mental Health, will analyze anorexia symptoms as they happen. Forty individuals with anorexia will use a hand-held computer, similar to a Palm Pilot, to record their symptoms. Subjects will carry the computer for two weeks.

Researchers are starting to collect test subjects for the study and will continue to do so for the next two years, Crow said.

"The advantage of this particular study is that it measures symptoms at the time they happen, rather than asking a patient about them three weeks later," he said.

Eventually, Crow said, the department hopes to develop new treatments from this data.

"You're more able to do that when you better understand the symptoms," he said.

Megan has been on and off of antidepressants to help control her binge eating since she started treatment two years ago. She had the eating habits under control for a while, but the stress of fall semester put her back on the pills.

Though it took some time, Megan is now comfortable taking antidepressants.

"I viewed them as a crutch," she said. "I didn't want to live my life taking meds.

"I decided I would much rather just be happy; I have to live with my thoughts every day."

Genes Contribute to Eating Disorders

Arline Kaplan

In the following article Arline Kaplan reports that genetic researchers have discovered a complex interplay between genes and the environment that leads to the development of eating disorders such as anorexia and bulimia. Kaplan reports that eating disorders are as strongly familial as schizophrenia and bipolar disorder, even though not every person with anorexia has a family member with anorexia. Nevertheless, studies of identical and fraternal twins that looked at three variances—genes, shared environment such as religion and economic status, and unique environment such as choice of sports and activities—revealed a high rate of heritability of anorexia and bulimia. Genes and unique environmental factors played the biggest role, while shared environment was less of a factor. Studies supported by the Price Foundation of Geneva identified possible areas on chromosomes for anorexia and bulimia. Arline Kaplan is senior contributing editor of *Psychiatric Times*.

SOURCE: *Psychiatric Times*, v. XXI, August 2004. Reproduced by permission.

Although eating disorders have been considered to be largely sociocultural in origin, findings from family, twin and molecular genetic studies conducted during the last decade are refuting that perspective, an expert in genetic epidemiology told attendees at the 2004 2nd World Congress on Women's Mental Health in Washington, D.C.

"Twenty years ago when I started in this field, and gave my favorite lecture on eating disorders, it was all about the role of the family and social factors in the etiology of eating disorders," said Cynthia M. Bulik, Ph.D., William R. and Jeanne H. Jordan Distinguished Professor of Eating Disorders in the department of psychiatry and director of the eating disorders program at the University of North Carolina, Chapel Hill.

"Both anorexia and bulimia were very much viewed as disorders of choice. These young girls were viewed as trying to emulate some cultural ideal and diet themselves down to a certain weight. Now, any patient would have told you had you listened that wasn't what they were doing. They went far beyond any societal ideal in *Cosmopolitan* or any other magazine," [said Bulik].

Bulik explained that when she and colleagues started talking about genes as being involved in these disorders, "people pretty much thought we were out of our minds." However, the investigators are discovering a complex interplay between genes and the environment leading to the development of anorexia nervosa (AN) and bulimia nervosa (BN). . . .

Eating Disorders Run in Families

[At the conference] Bulik continued with a brief description of genetic epidemiology, which looks at how genes and environment influence the risk for specific disorders. The first question asked is whether eating disorders run in families. If the answer to the family studies is that the disorder does run in families, the next step is twin

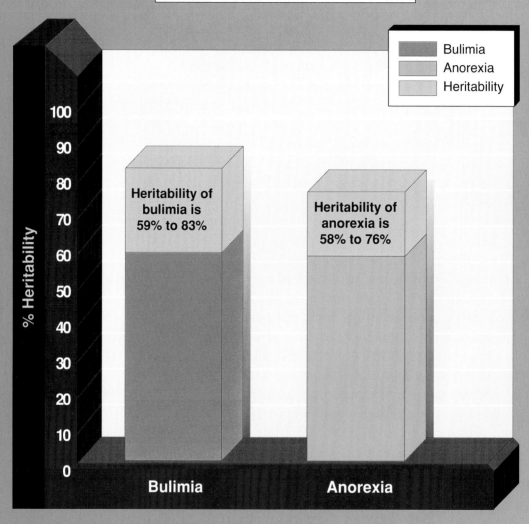

Percentage of Heritability

- Bulimia
- Anorexia
- Heritability

Heritability of bulimia is 59% to 83%

Heritability of anorexia is 58% to 76%

% Heritability

Bulimia

Anorexia

Source: *Psyciatric Times*, v. XXI, August 2004. Reproduced by permission.

and adoption studies to help determine the extent to which the disorder is due to genes or the environment. If genes are determined to be important, the researchers move on to conducting linkage and association studies to identify where the genes are and what they do.

Both AN and BN are strongly familial and are, in fact, as familial as schizophrenia and bipolar disorder, Bulik said.

"They don't breed true, in that a patient with anorexia doesn't only have family members with anorexia. You will see a mixture of eating disorders among the family members—bulimia, eating disorders [not otherwise specified] and threshold eating disorder behaviors. But relatives of individuals with eating disorders are at seven to 12 times higher risk than relatives of individuals without eating disorders. The familiality of anorexia nervosa is the highest; they tend to have the densest family history," she said.

Genetic Studies of Twins

While there are no published adoption studies for AN or BN, Bulik said, twin studies do exist. In twin studies, researchers compare concordance rates (the frequency with which both members of the twin pair have the disorder or the trait of interest). They compare those concordance rates in monozygotic [identical] and dizygotic [fraternal] twins.

Bulik explained that eating disorders are complex, and investigators know they are looking for multiple genes and environmental factors. To do that, the investigators are going beyond concordance rates in twins and looking at three different pockets of variance. [One is] the additive effect of genes. [The second is] shared environmental effects, such as family religion, parental rearing style or socioeconomic status in which the twin pair was raised.

[The third is] unique environmental effects, those things that happen in the environment that will influence one of the twins but not the other. For example, one of the twins joins a gymnastic club where an incompetent coach pressures her to diet to an unrealistic weight, while the other twin joins a soccer team where weight is not a major issue.

"When we started to do twin studies, we were all surprised, given that we had all grown up in that sociocultural tradition of eating disorders. When we look at those three pockets of variance, we actually find that the heritability of bulimia nervosa, for example, is somewhere between 59% and 83%. So what we are saying is the liability for developing bulimia nervosa is predominately affected by genetic factors. Shared environment wasn't terribly important."

"The remainder of risk comes out in those unique environmental factors. . . ." Bulik said. "Similar results came for anorexia nervosa—with the heritability of 58% to 76%. Again, shared environment wasn't terribly important, and the unique environment seemed to influence risk for anorexia nervosa."

Several population-based twin studies conducted around the world, primarily on individuals with European ancestry, have similarly concluded that AN and BN, as well as related phenotypes such as perfectionism, body dissatisfaction and drive for thinness, are moderately heritable, Bulik indicated.

Markers on Chromosomes Linked to Eating Disorders

A series of multisite studies supported by the Price Foundation of Geneva have helped identify possible areas on chromosome 1 for AN and areas on chromosome 10 for BN that may harbor susceptibility loci [locations] for these disorders.

Bulik described some of the studies in which she was an investigator, along with many others. . . .

"[One] study we did involved 192 individuals with anorexia nervosa and their affected relatives," said Bulik. "The probands [person being studied] had anorexia nervosa, but the family members could have had a whole cluster of eating disorder diagnoses. . . .

FAST FACT

People that have a family history of eating disorders are twelve times likelier to develop an eating disorder than the general population.

"...We found two genes ... one related to the serotonergic [serotonin] system and one related to opioidergic [opioids] system that may influence risk for anorexia nervosa," Bulik said. ...

Investigators are looking for genes that may influence proteins that may influence perfectionism, harm avoidance, appetite regulation, ease of vomiting, anxiety (a common premorbid [pre-disease] condition in people with eating disorders), obsessionality, high activity, obesity risk and binge eating, Bulik added.

"To complicate matters, we may have protective alleles [genes on a chromosome], traits that protect against the expression of these risk alleles, like genes that influence

Walter Kay, director of a team of eating disorder researchers getting $10 million to study anorexia in the hopes of finding genetic links. (AP Images)

self-esteem or genes that influence constitutional fitness. A couple of studies we have done show that individuals who tended to be thin all their lives are at much lower risk for eating disorders," she said. "Then you throw environmental factors in the mix, including protective factors such as breast-feeding. Unpacking the complexity of all these genetic and environmental factors is quite a task and also quite a challenge."

Once the investigators find the genes, they can use that information to better understand how the genes and environment interact. . . .

The most simple way to look at this is that a genotype might influence who is sensitive to the impact of that first unhealthy weight loss diet they go on, she said.

"To pull this all together, we need to look beyond nature versus nurture and pay greater attention to gene-environment interplay. Genetics research really enhances our ability to understand the role of environment," Bulik added. . . .

New Study Analyzes Birth and Risk of Eating Disorders

Bulik said she and colleagues are planning to start a study in Norway looking at 100,000 births and the risk of eating disorders. "We have extensive nutritional data on the women. We also have fetal ultrasounds, so we can look at growth in utero, and we have pregnancy outcome variables.

"The children are going to be followed up throughout adulthood, so we are going to be able to look at them through the ages where they are at risk for developing the disorder. But we can also go back and look at the maternal birth records of the moms, to see how many of the babies were premature, small for their gestational age, or other sorts of problems with labor and delivery. It will enable us to explore the cycle of risk across two generations in 100,000 births," she said.

"So we are saying that perinatal [around the time of birth] events are not exclusively environmental, a genetic tendency toward anorexia may influence inadequate weight gain during pregnancy. It also underscores the importance of prenatal monitoring in pregnant women with current or past eating disorders in order to interrupt the cycle of risk."

The Norwegian study, Bulik added, "might really help us unravel that nexus where genes and environment collide."

Families Cause Eating Disorders

Mark Dombeck

According to Mark Dombeck in the following article, family dynamics are an important contributing source of eating disorders. Dombeck claims that dysfunctional families may include parents who are overly involved in their children's lives, controlling or closely following their children's daily activities. These parents unwittingly encourage low self-esteem in their children, who respond by seeking control over their food intake and seeking their own identity, the author concludes. Children and teenagers may also learn eating habits from watching or emulating family members who have eating disorders. In addition, the author believes that other family issues, such as physical or mental abuse and drug or alcohol abuse, may lead children to develop eating disorders. Mark Dombeck, PhD, is director of MentalHelp.net and a licensed psychologist in the state of Ohio.

There is more to eating disorders than inherited genetics, personality and coping deficits. These factors interact in a complex way with behaviors

SOURCE: Mark Dombeck, "Causes of Eating Disorders—Family Influence," MentalHelp.net, February 2, 2007. Reproduced by permission.

learned from families and other important role models. In other words, researchers suspect that various family factors also play an important role in creating and maintaining eating disorders.

Children Learn Attitudes about Eating from Family

Social Learning Theory, coined and developed by psychologist Albert Bandura, suggests that development is highly influenced by our environment. As we grow up, we learn from family values as well as by watching what our parents model for us. Therefore, many children and young teenagers learn attitudes about eating and their bodies through observation, particularly from watching the adults in their lives. Children with parents who cope with emotional stress by using disordered eating mistakenly learn that this behavior is acceptable.

A family's eating habits have great influence over that of the children. (AP Images)

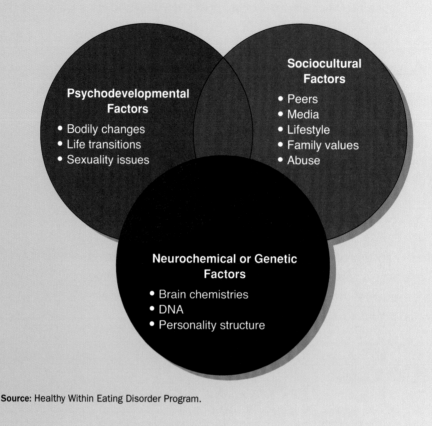

Various Causes Come Together to Create Disease

Psychodevelopmental Factors
- Bodily changes
- Life transitions
- Sexuality issues

Sociocultural Factors
- Peers
- Media
- Lifestyle
- Family values
- Abuse

Neurochemical or Genetic Factors
- Brain chemistries
- DNA
- Personality structure

Source: Healthy Within Eating Disorder Program.

Much of the research on eating disorders has focused on the development of healthy emotional boundaries in families. Researchers have found that, in some cases, families are over-involved and enmeshed with an individual who has an eating disorder.

"Enmeshed" is a psychological term describing a symbiotic and overly-intimate relationship in which the emotional and psychological boundaries between two people are so obscure or unclear that it is difficult for them to function as separate individuals with their own identities. Enmeshment generally develops slowly and typically does not erupt into conflict until the child becomes an adolescent, wanting to assert their independence and develop an identity outside of the family.

Overly Involved Parents Share Their Children's Identity

Teenagers in an enmeshed relationship may feel so powerless to develop a separate identity from an over-involved parent that they try to exert independence and autonomy by controlling what happens to their bodies.

Take for example, an adolescent girl who wants to join her high school cheerleading squad, which would require her to be away from home after school for daily practices. This separation may be emotionally threatening to an over-involved parent, who compensates by sharing the cheerleading identity with her daughter via attendance at daily practices, games and any related social gatherings. The daughter is unable to develop an identity separate from her mother, so she tries to exert control the only way she knows how, by controlling her food intake. This type of behavior can slowly develop into an eating disorder.

Research also indicates that families of individuals with eating disorders tend to be overprotective, perfectionistic, rigid, and focused on success. They have high, sometimes unreasonable expectations for achievement and may place exaggerated attention on external rewards. Many children from these kinds of families try to achieve the appearance of success by being thin and attractive, even if they do not feel successful. If children perceive that they are failing to live up to family expectations, they may turn to something that seems more easily controlled and at which they may be more successful, such as food restriction or weight loss.

> **FAST FACT**
>
> Exposure to stress in the forms of abuse, neglect, or loss of a parent during one's childhood increases the risk of behavioral and emotional problems such as anxiety, depression, suicide, and drug abuse—phenomena frequently associated with eating disorders—in teenagers and young adults.

Dysfunctional Families and Abuse Contribute to Eating Disorders

Pathology within the family may also contribute to eating disorders. Many individuals with eating disorders live in or came from families that exhibited dysfunctional or negative behaviors, such as alcohol and drug use. Marital discord, domestic violence and divorce are also not uncommon family issues for those suffering with an eating disorder. In addition, some people turn to an eating disorder after they've experienced a family trauma such as sexual or physical abuse, or neglect. Individuals who have experienced significant trauma may also develop Post Traumatic Stress Disorder, a debilitating condition that follows a frightening and often life-threatening event causing severe anxiety, flashbacks, and unwanted, repeated frightening memories or thoughts of the event.

Families Do Not Cause Eating Disorders

Kelli McElhinny

In the following article Kelli McElhinny explains that a genetic predisposition toward eating disorders is the real cause of the illness, not unsupportive or dysfunctional families. Since a very small percentage of women and men develop an eating disorder, societal pressure alone cannot be the cause, McElhinny contends. These pressures may only trigger a latent genetic risk for the disease. The author contends that misstatements about families causing eating disorders may prevent sufferers from getting help and may prevent insurance companies from treating a nonbiological illness. Researchers from a National Institute of Mental Health–funded study are conducting a nationwide study on the role of genes in anorexia nervosa. Kelli McElhinny is a writer and the media coordinator of the University of Pittsburgh Medical Center.

Misstatements and ignorance claiming that families "cause" eating disorders is like blaming parents for diabetes or asthma or cancer, says an

SOURCE: Kelli McElhinny, "Families Do Not Cause Anorexia Nervosa," *Medical News Today*, January 25, 2007. 2006 © MediLexicon International Ltd. Reproduced by permission.

international group of eating disorders researchers. Recent damaging statements by fashion model Gisele Bundchen stating that unsupportive families cause anorexia nervosa only perpetuate misconceptions and further stigmatize eating disorders.

Contrary to her claim, there is no scientific evidence that families cause anorexia nervosa. In fact, the researchers are finding that anorexia nervosa is far more complex than simply wanting to be slim to achieve some

A happy, well adjusted family can help keep eating disorders at bay through a family support system.
(AP Images)

fashionable slender ideal. The data show that anorexia nervosa has a strong genetic component that may be the root cause of this illness.

"An uninformed opinion such as Bundchen's causes harm on a number of levels. By contributing to the stigma, it drives sufferers underground and creates obstacles to seeking help. It damages attempts at advocacy and hurts parents who are desperately fighting for their child's recovery," said Allan S. Kaplan, M.D., Loretta Anne Rogers Chair in Eating Disorders at the University of Toronto. "Such thinking also misinforms third party payors who may not want to pay for the treatment of these biologically-based illnesses if they think its primary cause is family dysfunction."

The Search for Anorexia's Genetic Link

Dr. Kaplan is a member of the international group of researchers attempting to find which genes contribute to anorexia nervosa through a National Institute of Mental Health–funded study of families with a history of anorexia nervosa. The current study, which is being conducted at 10 sites across the world, hopes to further clarify which genes play a role in anorexia nervosa. The study builds on data from 10 years of groundbreaking research on the genetics of eating disorders sponsored by the Price Foundation.

"We often hear that societal pressures to be thin cause many young women and men to develop an eating disorder. Many individuals in our culture, for a number of reasons, are concerned with their weight and diet. Yet less than half of 1 percent of all women develop anorexia nervosa, which indicates to us that societal pressure alone isn't enough to cause someone to develop this disease," said Walter H. Kaye, M.D., professor of psychiatry, University of Pittsburgh School of Medicine.

"Our research has found that genes seem to play a substantial role in determining who is vulnerable to developing an eating disorder. However, the societal pressure isn't irrelevant; it may be the environmental trigger that releases a person's genetic risk. Families should not be blamed for causing anorexia. In fact, they are often devastated and suffer from the consequences of this illness," [said Kaye].

High Mortality Rate for Anorexia Sufferers

Anorexia nervosa is a serious and potentially lethal illness, with a mortality rate greater than 10 percent. It is characterized by the relentless pursuit of thinness, emaciation and the obsessive fear of gaining weight. Anorexia nervosa commonly begins during adolescence, but strikes throughout the lifespan—it is nine times more

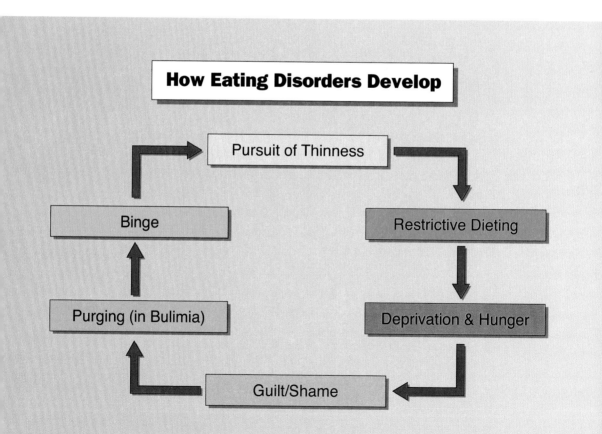

Source: American Intitute for Cognitive Therapy. www.cognitivetherapynyc.com/problems.asp?sid=251.

common in females than in males. Personality traits, such as perfectionism, anxiety and obsessionality, are often present in childhood before the eating disorder develops and may contribute to the risk of developing this disorder.

"We need to understand all the factors that influence eating disorders, both genetic and environmental, and find ways to address them in order to prevent people from developing these potentially deadly conditions," said Cynthia Bulik, Ph.D., William and Jeanne Jordan Distinguished Professor of Eating Disorders, University of North Carolina at Chapel Hill.

"Understanding how genes and environment interact both to increase risk for eating disorders and to protect those who are genetically vulnerable from developing the disorder will require the cooperation of professionals in the eating disorders field, the media, and the fashion and entertainment industries. Only cooperatively, will we be able to move the field forward toward the elimination of this disease," [said Bulik].

"Anorexia nervosa has the highest death rate of any mental illness, yet so few dollars are dedicated to the cure," stated Lynn Grefe, CEO of the National Eating Disorders Association. "These scientific advances demonstrating a genetic component are significant and so meaningful to our families, wiping away the myths and emphasizing the need for even more research to help the next generation."

> **FAST FACT**
>
> Research has discovered hormonal disturbances and imbalances of neurotransmitters in the brain that can regulate mood and appetite.

The Fashion Industry Is Responsible for Policing Models' Eating Disorders

Elizabeth Wellington

In the following article fashion writer Elizabeth Wellington believes that the fashion industry should take responsibility for the image it is giving young women when it presents superskinny models and a body image that is impossible to attain. Despite the deaths of models in Milan, Italy, and Barcelona, Spain, suffering from anorexia, Wellington explains that the Council of Fashion Designers of America has refused to take responsibility for policing its models' eating disorders and will not ban models with a low body mass index. Fashion designers are a business and are more concerned with making garments they perceive as beautiful, and they will continue to show these clothes on very thin models, Wellington concludes. Elizabeth Wellington is a fashion writer for the *Philadelphia Inquirer* and was previously the fashion writer for the *News and Observer* in Raleigh, North Carolina.

We all know models are thin, often painfully so. It's evident here at Fall Fashion Week, under way ... at the tents in Bryant Park [Manhattan], as you watch them skulk down the runway, bones protruding through their milky skin. It's jarring.

The health of these models has become a worldwide issue, as the fashion industry has finally been clued in to the fact that young girls look up to models and sometimes do whatever it takes to achieve their small frames and nonexistent waistlines.

Late last year, fashion-show organizers in Milan and Barcelona set guidelines to try to prevent models with anorexia nervosa, bulimia and other eating disorders from appearing on the runways. Paris and London fashion bigwigs have also discussed the issue.

Council of Fashion Designers of America Committee

To show that American designers care about the welfare of their models, Seventh Avenue's Council of Fashion Designers of America (CFDA) discussed the problem over a low-carb breakfast of coffee, yogurt parfait and tiny pastries Monday morning [in February 2007].

Designer Diane von Furstenberg, president of the CFDA, stated that the fashion industry cannot take the full responsibility for policing models' eating disorders.

"But we should project health as part of beauty and be sensitive to it," she said, adding that all of the CFDA's 283 members were behind the initiative. "I'm happy this issue has been raised."

The breakfast symposium featured a committee of five, including a nutritionist, a weight trainer, and Susan Ice, medical director of the Renfrew Center of Philadelphia, a residential treatment facility for eating disorders.

> ## FAST FACT
>
> The average woman is 5 feet 4 inches tall and weighs 140 pounds, while the average female model is 5 feet 11 inches tall and weighs 117 pounds.

Designers Donna Karan and Philadelphia native Tory Burch were also in attendance.

The experts offered suggestions to promote healthier industry standards, such as raising the runway models' minimum age to 16, identifying models who have developed or are in danger of developing eating disorders, and

The fashion industry plays a major role in a girl's self-image. **(AP Images)**

Body Mass Index (BMI)

Body mass index, or BMI, is a new term to most people. However, it is the measurement of choice for many physicians and researchers studying obesity. BMI uses a mathematical formula that takes into account both a person's height and weight. BMI equals a person's weight in kilograms divided by height in meters squared. ($BMI = kg/m^2$).

BMI	Risk of Associated Disease According to BMI and Waist Size	Waist less than or equal to 40 in. (men) or 35 in. (women)	Waist greater than 40 in. (men) or 35 in. (women)
18.5 or less	Underweight	--	N/A
18.5 - 24.9	Normal	--	N/A
25.0 - 29.9	Overweight	Increased	High
30.0 - 34.9	Obese	High	Very High
35.0 - 39.9	Obese	Very High	Very High
40 or greater	Extremely Obese	Extremely High	Extremely High

Source: Partnership for Healthy Weight Management. www.consumer.gov/weightloss/bmi.htm.

requiring counseling for models who have an unhealthy relationship with food.

Designers were also encouraged to provide plenty of water and healthy snacks for the models backstage, while forbidding smoking and drinking.

Minimum Body Mass Index for Models

But the American experts failed to take the more drastic regulatory step that is dividing the fashion world: setting a minimum Body Mass Index, or BMI, for working models.

That's what fashion-show organizers in Spain and Italy did last year [2006]. There, women who have a BMI of less than 18 cannot model, because they are likely suffering from an eating disorder. (A woman who is 5-foot-10 would have to weigh 125 pounds to have a BMI of 18.)

Joy Bauer, founder of the Joy Bauer Nutritional Center in New York, disagreed with the BMI minimums, saying that the number is not an indicator of overall health.

Bauer, who works with models to show them how to maintain modeling weight, said that it is possible for a woman to have a BMI of 14 and be healthy.

"This issue is more than about BMI and weight," Bauer said. "It's about getting models more comfortable with food."

(A 5-foot-10 woman with a BMI of 14 would weigh 100 pounds or less.)

The designers also balked at setting guidelines for themselves on the types of clothes they create. Typically, sample sizes at Fashion Week are made for very thin women.

"We do not feel it is our scope or our job to tell designers what kind of clothes they should design or choose what body shape best shows those clothes," said Nian Fish, the creative director of KCD, a New York–based public relations firm that represents designers such as Zac Posen during Fashion Week.

"This is their aesthetic choice."

Designers Want Size 2 Models

And this is where the CFDA's intentions, no matter how well-meaning, fall flat.

As the drumbeat for healthier models grows louder (former supermodel Tyra Banks, who now weighs 160 pounds, just appeared on her talk show and on the cover of *People* in a bathing suit, railing against the very thin standards that she herself upheld in her youth), the organization finds itself in a precarious situation.

It represents designers' rights, after all, one of which is to design garments beautiful in their own eyes.

Nonetheless, the unfortunate fact remains that these images promote a sense of desperation, for the models themselves and for the women who look at them and try to achieve a body that is impossible to attain.

"Designers want people a size 2 or 4," said Pamela Lankford, owner of the Philadelphia-based modeling agency Expressions. "They are looking at hangers for their clothing. They feel the thinner the model is, the better the clothes drape on the model."

The surprising thing is that most designers are not pencil-thin themselves.

Tracy Reese, for example, presents wonderful clothing. This season, her trapeze dresses in tangerine, along with hot trench coats in chocolate brown, were phenomenal. But her models were tiny.

Alice Roi, whose punk rock-meets-sophisticated look focused on mod black and white styles, also showed her collection on twig-thin models. . . .

Some Designs for Women Above Size 2

Now it just needs to be clear—to models as well as to the rest of us— that it's OK to be bigger than a size 2 to fill them up.

The Fashion Industry Takes Steps to Discourage Models' Eating Disorders

Council of Fashion Designers of America

Officials of the Council of Fashion Designers of America (CFDA) announce in the following article that, while fashion designers do share a responsibility to protect the women who work in their industry, they are not responsible for eating disorders among their models. Eating disorders are a complex issue encompassing psychological, behavioral, social, and physical elements, says the CFDA. The council contends that it will not recommend that models consult a doctor to assess their health and will not require a body mass index reading on models before they are permitted to work. However, the CFDA has formed a committee to propose a health initiative that will educate models on warning signs of eating disorders, develop workshops on identifying and treating eating disorders, and promote healthy eating habits backstage and during photo shoots.

The Council of Fashion Designers of America (CFDA) recently formed a health initiative to address what has become a global fashion issue: the overwhelming concern about whether some models are unhealthily thin, and whether or not to impose restrictions in such cases. Designers share responsibility to protect women, and very young girls in particular, within the business, sending the message that beauty is health. While some models are naturally tall and thin and their appearance is a result of many factors, including genetics, youth, nutritional food, and exercise, other models have or develop eating disorders.

CFDA Committee to Promote Wellness

Although we cannot fully assume responsibility for an issue that is as complex as eating disorders and that occurs

New York state assemblyman Jose Rivera (left) has proposed legislation demanding that the fashion industry stick to weight guidelines. (AP Images)

in many walks of life, the fashion industry can begin a campaign of awareness and create an atmosphere that supports the well-being of these young women. Working in partnership with the fashion industry, medical experts, nutritionists, and fitness trainers, the CFDA has formed a committee to propose a series of positive steps designed to promote wellness and a healthier working environment. We recognize that change will take time and are committed to industry-specific educational efforts, awareness programs, support systems, and evaluation and treatment options that advance our recommendations.

Recommendations for Educating Models

- Educate the industry to identify the early warning signs in an individual at risk of developing an eating disorder.
- Require models who are identified as having an eating disorder . . . to seek professional help in order to continue modeling. And models who are receiving professional help for an eating disorder should not continue modeling without that professional's approval.
- Develop workshops for the industry (including models and their families) on the nature of eating disorders, how they arise, how we identify and treat them, and complications if they are untreated.
- Support the well-being of younger individuals by not hiring models under the age of sixteen for runway shows; not allowing models under the age of eighteen to work past midnight at fittings or shoots; and providing regular breaks and rest.
- Supply healthy meals, snacks, and water backstage and at shoots and provide nutrition and fitness education.
- Promote a healthy backstage environment by raising the awareness of the impact of smoking and tobacco-related disease among women, ensuring a smoke-free

Dieting and the Drive for Thinness

42 percent of first and third grade girls want to be thinner (Collins, 1991).

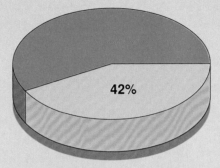

81 percent of ten-year-olds are afraid of being fat (Mellin et al., 1991).

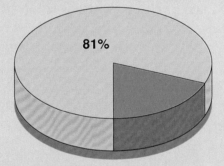

The average American woman is 5'4" tall and weighs 140 pounds. The average American model is 5'11" tall and weighs 117 pounds.

Most fashion models are thinner than 98 percent of American women (Smolak, 1996).

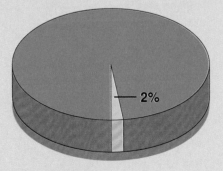

Source: National Eating Disorders Association. www.edap.org.

environment, and address underage drinking by pro-
hibiting alcohol.

CFDA Will Not Police Models

The CFDA Health Initiative is about awareness and education, not policing. Therefore, the committee is not
recommending that models get a doctor's
physical examination to assess their health
or body-mass index to be permitted to
work. Eating disorders are emotional disorders that have psychological, behavioral, social, and physical manifestations, of which
body weight is only one.

> **FAST FACT**
>
> Celebrities who have strug-
> gled with eating disorders
> include Princess Diana,
> Elton John, Paula Abdul,
> Whitney Houston, Elvis
> Presley, and Oprah Winfrey.

The CFDA Health Initiative is committed to the notion of a healthy mind in a
healthy body, and there cannot be one without the other. The industry is determined
to foster a balanced approach to nutrition,
recreation, exercise, work, and relationships. In support of our recommendations, the CFDA will
present a discussion on health and beauty during Fashion Week on February 5 [2007] to an audience composed
of designers, models, agents, editors, and industry lead-
ers, along with representatives from eating-disorder organizations, nutritionists, and other health professionals.

The Internet Promotes Eating Disorders

Jill Meredith Collins

Young girls are surrounded by images of thin, beautiful women, caus-ing these girls to think that they need to be thin in order to be beau-tiful. This fixation on weight can result in deadly eating disorders. Unfortunately, some people do not view eating disorders in a nega-tive light, resulting in the disturbing trend of proeating disorder Web sites. Pro-ana (anorexia) and pro-mia (bulimia) sites provide online journaling about eating disorder behaviors, including how to perpet-uate the disorder and how to hide it from others, giving dangerous advice to impressionable young women. Jill Meredith Collins is a writer for the feminist news journal *Off Our Backs*.

It's a typical day in 21st century America. All our doors are locked. Our children are boarding school buses in hopes of being the bully and not the bullied as they make their way down the road to say the pledge of allegiance, with or without the words "under God."

SOURCE: Jill Meredith Collins, "Nurturing Destruction: Eating Disorders Online." *Off Our Backs,* November/December 2004.

Katie Couric, Matt Lauer and Al Roker [hosts of NBC's *The Today Show*] are reporting from the Rockefeller Plaza while tourists wave signs outside of it. And our young girls nervously walk into the halls of their high schools worrying about how much they ate for breakfast.

The Desire to Be Skinny

It's a typical day for an adolescent female. She wakes up and notices whether or not she's hungry, eats a light, fat-free breakfast if she thinks she's too hungry to make it until lunch, which she'll probably skip so she can eat a full dinner so as not to worry her parents. She is surrounded by images of thin women, and she knows that all women don't look like Christina Aguilera [pop singer], but her subconscious registers her own body type as being something other than beautiful. If her jeans fit a little more tightly than they did the day before, she feels like crying. If she manages to shed a few pounds, she'll be praised for it by peers and even adults. The teen magazines that she looks to for guidance warn her of eating disorders, but they show pictures of girls who are little more than skeletons, while the opposite page shows a 100-pound model who could just as easily be undernourished. She knows the danger, and yet she wonders, how hard would it be to just let it happen? Be skinny, be praiseworthy, get attention . . . even if that attention ends up being medical attention.

It may sound ridiculous, but the longing to give in to anorexia is frighteningly common. As the ever-foolish media attempts to educate young girls of the danger, they accidentally glamorize the disease. I vividly remember the TV movies "For the Love of Nancy" and "A Secret Between Friends," which were used in my health classes to educate us, in hopes that we would not develop eating

> **FAST FACT**
>
> A 2005 survey of adolescent anorexics and their parents found that 39 percent of the kids visited pro-ana Web sites.

disorders. Incidentally, these movies show exactly how it is done—how these girls hide their food and cover their tracks, and the unwavering dedication that they possess.

This kind of education takes place at the age when young girls crave drama in their lives. If you have a horrible life, at least you know that you have a life. Girls crave validation. Tragedy romanticizes existence, and this is exactly what young girls want: a romantic existence. This sort of romanticizing brings up the issue of control, the issue most often used as an umbrella reason for eating disorders. You can't be in every movie, you can't make a handsome prince fall in love with you, you can't fly over the rainbow—but you can develop an eating disorder. All you have to do is follow the steps taken by the girl in the movie.

When I watched these movies in my early teenage years, I couldn't help but notice the concern friends and family held for the girl in question. They looked out for her, took care of her, and there was no doubt that they sincerely loved her. I couldn't help but wonder if anyone loved me that much. If I ever became anorexic, would someone be there to help me through it? I needed my family and friends to prove their love to me. I didn't consciously develop anorexia because of this need, but I admit that I formed the idea.

The Rise of Pro-ana and Pro-mia Web Sites

It is because of my memories of life in the impressionable pre-anorexic mind that I worry about the generation of girls growing up after me. The images of females in the media haven't changed since then. In fact, probably the only major change in the media in the past ten years has been the rise of Internet usage. And this combination of factors has resulted in a very disturbing trend: pro-anorexia websites. Or, as the sites like to call themselves, "pro-ana." When they refer to bulimia, then it's "mia." Eating disorders in general are simply shortened to "eds." Another word that has been coined for this phenomenon is "thinspiration," which usually involves pictures of extremely thin women, both models and clinically thin victims of anorexia.

The Eating Disorders Association believes at least 400 pro-anorexia sites and chatrooms currently exist on the Internet. The content of the sites usually consists of online journaling about anorexic behaviors and comments on the journaling. Girls exchange tips on how to perpetuate the disorder and how to hide it from others. The most popular tagline is "Anorexia is a lifestyle, not a disease."

The sites generally operate under the pretense of support, and some of them may actually accomplish that for girls who are already anorexic and do not intend to recover. The question is whether support for their state is actually a good thing. Some of the contributors say they "suffer" from "ana," while others relish it and say they enjoy it. They refuse help in getting better. But very few eating disorder victims are willing to go into recovery until someone intervenes and insists on it (in my case, it was my mother). Some of the sites want to help minimize the damage to the body; others are overtly harmful. They naively believe that their words do not influence others, but I have read the following sentence on an online diary: "I think I might cut up my gums so it hurts to eat so I won't want to; I saw that on a pro-ana site." This statement is proof of at least one instance where the sites have been used as instructional.

Pro-ana Sites Offer Dangerous Reinforcement

Many other anorexic girls, however, wander into these "anorexic communities" looking for support in conquering something that is on the verge of destroying them. They do not get the help they need from the proanorexia websites; instead they get reinforcement of the problem

that they want to overcome. In that stage, it's very difficult to overcome something when others are convincing
you that you don't need to. I remember the "you've lost
weight" compliments when I was very sick, and how they
made me struggle with whether to recover at all. I always
told myself that the givers of these compliments had no
idea what they were saying because they did not know I
was anorexic. These memories convince me that someone knowing you were anorexic, and still reinforcing it,
could easily drive a young girl over the edge.

Teenage girls are
especially vulnerable
to society's standards
of what is considered
pretty, even when the
role models are sick
with an eating
disorder. (AP Images)

A number of "pro-ana" communities exist on the popular LiveJournal.com server. One such community states on its profile, "This is a supportive community for anorexies and bulimics. This is not a debate community and there will be no bashing of our views. This community is especially created for thinspiration such as thinspiring pictures or poems or stories. All are welcome." The comment on bashing of their views seems to be echoed in the profile of another community:

"If you are anti-ed, then you are NOT welcome here. How about you all stop treating people with eds like little children who don't know any better? We know the health side effects because we live with them everyday [sic]. I think it's cruel that you all make jokes at people with eating disorder's expense and then try to justify it by saying you just want them to be happy and eat and healthy. You just want someone to attack and belittle is what your problem is. I don't want to hear about society. What else do you morons ever say? And quit stalking ed related communities. Some people are happy at their weight but we are not. So go away. Don't bother to join this community and post bullshit because I'll delete and remove you faster than you can wipe your ass."

Reading this reveals a hurt and angry person with a strong enough command of language to make her argument effective. Yet I can't look away from the name of the community: "fat ana: overweight with ed." The page's background shows a girl who looks perfectly healthy standing atop a scale, as if to imply that she is overweight.

Diary Entries

One LiveJournal user writes on the "anti-ana" community that she fled to it from the "pro-ana" communities:

"I'm documenting my recovery, because it was so hard for me to find resources that dealt with the actual recovery. I would go into chat rooms seeking advice and most of the girls there would get into contests to see who was 'sicker.' Oh my God, you're a candidate for inpatient? I wish I was that sick!!' I left those in absolute disgust."

One owner of a pro-anorexia diary writes as her introduction,

"I live my life in the pursuit of being thinner. I've been doing this since my 16th birthday; it's like on that day I realized how fat I was. I was 120 lbs and thought nothing of it, but little did I realize I was on the road to being just like the rest of my family . . . severly [sic] obese. I vowed that day to be skinny, and I'm still working on it. I've long since passed my original weight loss goals, yet when I look into the mirror, I still see a fat girl looking back. I can't stop now, I must be as thin as I possibly can. And I will do whatever it takes to get there."

Chills run down my spine. One-hundred-twenty is a healthy weight for an adolescent female, and doing whatever it takes to be as thin as possible will, ultimately, end in death.

The Fatality Factor

The fatality factor seems to be ignored by these sites. I have even seen one that was "in memory of _____ who died of anorexia. She was an avid pro-anorexic." The logic in that baffles me. When someone dies of AIDS, we don't try to help AIDS patients stay sick. What would we say if people with heart disease had online communities where they egged each other on in eating Big Macs? One member of a proanorexia forum offers "fasting" tips, then wraps them up by saying, "BUT MOST IMPORTANT: If you die, all your hard work is USELESS. So don't die, ok? Cause I'll miss you!"

Many personal web page servers, such as Angelfire and Yahoo, have banned pro-anorexic sites on the domains which they sponsor. The majority of the proanorexic sites that thrive are on online diary services such as LiveJournal and Diaryland. Many people suspect that the websites exist for shock value and attention-getting, which is a viable theory considering the overtly rough language and seemingly ignorant stance of the "pro-ana" sites.

Pro-ana Sites Attract Many Viewers

Naturally, pro-anorexia sites catch the eyes of many concerned individuals such as myself. I have been brave enough to approach the sites with comments along the lines of "please understand that anorexia is a serious disease. I suffered it myself, and I strongly encourage you

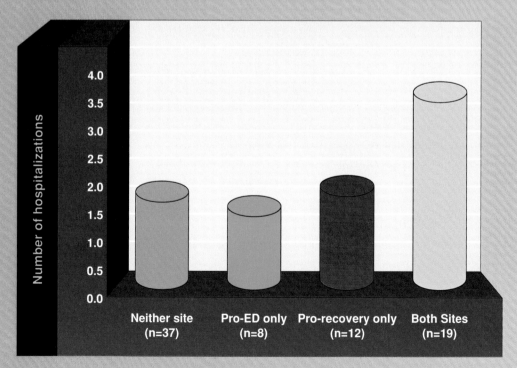

Hazards of Visiting ED Web Sites

Number of hospitalizations among users of neither pro-ED nor pro-recovery sites, users of pro-ED sites but not pro-recovery sites, users of pro-recovery but not pro-ED sites, and users of both sites.

Source: National Eating Disorders Association, www.edap.org.

to get help. Please think about the effect that your website could have on people." Most of these comments go ignored, not surprisingly. Although I did receive one rewarding reply thanking me for my concern and the inspiration of my recovery, most of the replies I've gotten are of this variety: "I am not going to turn some girl into an anorexic. Do you think I am an idiot to all of a sudden change what I write to please you? You proboly [sic] cut and paste that line on tons of journals just so you can get some sort of peace of mind. Well, you look like a dumbass." And maybe I do look like a dumbass. But I'm okay with that. What I'm not okay with is sitting idly by and watching, unable to look away from the screen as if it were a terrible car crash.

It terrifies me to think about what would have happened if I had seen these sites just a few short years ago. I am saddened and disgusted that the consciousness of our culture has led not only to breeding eating disorders in young girls, but now in allowing them to purposely nurture one another's harmful behavior. These are our young girls, and this is the world they are growing up in. They believe themselves to be adults, beyond a need for guidance—but who among us remembers being fifteen and impressionable? Who among us is glad that our distorted self-destructive notions were not encouraged any further than they were? Who among us is glad to still be here today, having won (or almost won) the battles we fought as a teenager? Maybe sites like these will always exist, but shouldn't we at least be making the effort to outweigh them with nurturing of another kind?

The Internet Provides Treatment for Eating Disorders

Sandra G. Boodman

In the following article Sandra G. Boodman of the *Washington Post* reports that an eight-week Internet-based study conducted by Stanford University aimed to reduce the occurrence of eating disorders in high-risk women. Nearly five hundred California college students participated in the study called "Student Bodies." Boodman reports that the program featured online sessions about healthy eating, journal writing, and interactive discussions monitored by a psychologist. Two subgroups among the women showed a significantly low level development of an eating disorder, compared to the control group, according to Boodman. The study's results prove that low-cost Internet-based programs for prevention of eating disorders are favorable to expensive treatment programs that generally have a low success rate once the disease takes root. Sandra G. Boodman is a staff writer for the *Washington Post*.

The programs have catchy names like "Food, Mood and Attitude" and "Full of Ourselves" as well as an ambitious goal: to prevent adolescent eating dis-

SOURCE: Sandra G. Boodman, "Bodies of Evidence," *The Washington Post*, October 31, 2006, p. HE01. Copyright © 2006, The Washington Post. Reprinted with permission.

orders, which tend to be chronic, difficult to treat and sometimes fatal.

But do they work?

In the case of one such program—"Student Bodies," developed by researchers at Stanford University—a recently published study suggests that the answer is yes. Stanford researchers, who followed 480 female California college students for up to two years, report that the eight-week Internet-based program reduced the development of eating disorders in women at high risk. "This study shows that innovative intervention can work," said Thomas Insel, director of the National Institute of Mental Health, which funded the study; its findings appeared in the August issue of the *Archives of General Psychiatry*.

Prevent the Disease in High-Risk Populations

Prevention programs for eating disorders have proliferated in the past decade, in part because of the high cost and low success rate of treatment programs. The disorders include a constellation of problems, including anorexia, a pathological fear of gaining weight marked by self-starvation. Anorexia has the highest mortality rate of any psychiatric illness: About 10 percent of patients hospitalized for treatment ultimately die of the disorder.

An estimated 4 percent of teenage girls and young women suffer from anorexia or bulimia, which is marked by recurrent binging and purging, or binge-eating disorder, in which sufferers gorge themselves until they become sick. Another 4 percent are believed to suffer from less severe subclinical forms of these disorders, which can last a lifetime and wreak physical and emotional havoc. The incidence of the disorders has doubled in the past 40 years, according to statistics compiled by the Eating Disorders Coalition, a Washington advocacy group.

"This study is a very significant piece of research because it demonstrates that one can transfer what's known

California colleges introduced a Web-based therapy system for college students with eating disorders. (**AP Images**)

about risk factors into a program that can be applied at very low cost," said Michael Levine, an eating disorders expert who is a professor of psychology at Kenyon College in Ohio. "And it gives every indication of being able to reduce important risk factors" for eating disorders such as excessive concern about body image and weight.

Computer-Based Program Raises Awareness

"I can't think of a single computer-based eating disorders program that can hold a candle to these results," said University of Texas psychologist Eric Stice, who two years ago conducted a meta-analysis and found that about 20 percent of eating disorders programs have a statistically significant benefit. Few programs, he said, have involved as many subjects or long-term follow-up as the Stanford approach. Programs achieving the best results, Stice said, are targeted at high-risk subjects rather than the general population of teenagers, involve girls 15 or over, and are interactive rather than didactic.

Clinicians say that effective prevention programs are badly needed. "These are very difficult problems to treat," said Sherry Goldman, a child psychiatrist and pediatrician who practices in Rockville [Maryland]. Many teenage eating disorder patients, she said, "don't recognize the seriousness of their symptoms" and don't think they have a problem.

It's not clear what causes eating disorders, which seem to run in families for reasons that may be biological or environmental—or both. The vast majority of sufferers are female, which experts say is partly a reflection of cultural norms such as the current popular fascination with skeletal-looking celebrities.

But few experts think culture alone is responsible. Goldman and others who treat teenage girls say that underlying depression is common in eating disorder patients, as are certain personality traits including competitiveness, conformity, rigidity and perfectionism. Many patients have difficulty expressing emotion; some have been sexually or physically abused as children. For them, eating—or not eating—becomes something they can control and a way of dissipating feelings that would otherwise be overwhelming.

FAST FACT

Funding for health care, and especially for eating disorders, has decreased in recent years, and the Internet provides opportunities for education, treatment, and prevention of eating disorders outside the realm of this missing funding.

Online Sessions and Interactive Discussions

Psychiatrist C. Barr Taylor, lead author of the Stanford study and a developer of "Student Bodies," said his team

Teenage Girls' Thoughts on Body Image

About 35–50 percent of teenage girls have a high level of concern about their weight and body shape.

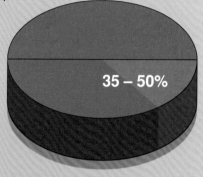

35 – 50%

An estimated 4 percent of teenage girls and young women suffer from anorexia or bulimia. Another 4 percent are believed to suffer from less severe subclinical forms of the disorders, which can last a lifetime.

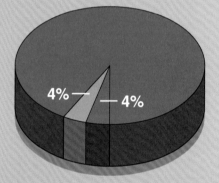

4% — — 4%

Anorexia has the highest mortality rate of any psychiatric illness: About 10 percent of patients hospitalized for treatment died of the disorder.

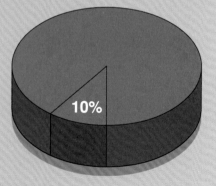

10%

Source: Sandra G. Boodman, "Bodies of Evidence," *Washington Post*, October 31, 2006.

focused on young women known to be especially susceptible to eating problems: the 35 to 50 percent of teenage
girls with high levels of concern about their weight and
body shape, some of whom were overweight. Among the
questions used to screen study participants was: "How
afraid are you of gaining three pounds?" Possible answers
included "moderately" and "very."

Through fliers posted at colleges in San Francisco
and San Diego, the team recruited 480 women whose average age was nearly 21 and whose average body mass
index (BMI) was 23.7—in the normal range, equivalent
to a 5-foot-4 woman who weighs 138 pounds.

Half were randomly assigned to "Student Bodies,"
which included weekly online sessions about healthy eating, journal keeping and an interactive discussion monitored by a psychologist, as well as information about
body image. The other half were assigned to a control
group and permitted to go through the program once
the evaluation was complete.

Reduced Development of Eating Disorders among High-Risk Groups

A two-year follow-up revealed no overall difference in
the development of eating disorders between the control
group and "Student Bodies" participants, Taylor said. But
it did find significant differences in two high-risk subgroups: students who were overweight and those who
were already engaged in behaviors that can presage a full-
blown disorder, such as excessive exercise, self-induced
vomiting and use of diet pills or laxatives.

Among "Student Bodies" participants with a BMI
over 25, which is considered overweight, none had developed an eating disorder at the two-year follow-up,
while 12 percent in the control group had.

And among the women from San Francisco (but not
San Diego) who reported problem behaviors such as self-
induced vomiting at the start of the study, 14 percent had

developed an eating disorder at the two-year mark, compared with 30 percent of the control group.

"We're the first study to show it's possible to prevent eating disorders among a high-risk group," Taylor said.

"Student Bodies" is not currently available as a prevention program, but Taylor said that its originators are considering offering it to other schools that have expressed interest.

"What's really novel about this program is that it's computer-administered and easy to disseminate," Stice said. "That's what makes it tantalizing."

CHAPTER 3

The Personal Side of Eating Disorders

d I am not. I feel guilty for not p
se If I stop they'll get mad—so I do
to do even though it brings mega
ay stop...   98.1 lbs

HATE MY BODY

stomach was all cquinched together
he Elastic in YOGA... stop... st
... I think I am Losing my mind...
ve to dive into this with Adam becau
talked about it so what do I have to
lot... I want a cigarette... SO
KAUE

CAMEL

99 4 lbs

A Woman Struggles with Anorexia

Cathleen Kronemer

In the following article exercise instructor Cathleen Kronemer, who was an overweight child, describes the onset of anorexia when she reached puberty. Concerned that she was "taking up space" and confronting a body that was changing as she approached adulthood, Kronemer greatly desired to take control of her life any way she could. This control took the form of anorexia. Realizing the disorder was harming her, she turned her attention to physical fitness, exercise, and weightlifting. She began to eat more protein to build muscle mass and to keep up her energy. Cathleen Kronemer is a group-exercise instructor certified by the Aerobics and Fitness Association of America. She runs a children's fitness company in St. Louis, Missouri.

Photo on previous page. Food diaries and personal journals are instrumental tools in defeating anorexia and bulimia. (AP Images)

"If you're not living on the edge, you're taking up too much space."
Anyone who has ever tried to embody these words, as a philosophy, is most likely aware of two things:

SOURCE: Cathleen Kronemer, "The Balance of Power," *American Fitness*, vol. 23, January-February 2005, pp. 53–54. Copyright © 2005 American Fitness Magazine. Reproduced by permission.

thrill and danger. Thrill can come in the manner of extreme sports, daredevil challenges and risks that leave you feeling exhilarated. But when the philosophy manifests itself as an eating disorder, the outcome can be deadly.

Desire to Take Control

I have struggled with anorexia for the past 30 years. The concept of "taking up space" as a negative entity began for me at 13. Poised on the brink of puberty, living in a body that was changing without my permission, I attempted to take control and stop the forces of nature by denying my body the nutrition it needed to evolve into adulthood. Taunted throughout childhood for being fat, it seemed like the perfect time to stop taking up so much space. I was going to call the shots now. Taking control, I reasoned, was somehow going to save me from a transition I was not prepared for.

Taking control—what a paradox that concept turned out to be. What started as me controlling what went into my mouth, down to the last calorie, quickly turned into a nightmare. Contrary to my belief system, I was no longer in control of my life; I was held captive by the eating disorder, which had taken on a soul of its own. Anorexia had me in its clutches; I had given it power over me, and it was making all the rules and decisions in my life. It dictated what I ate, how many sit-ups I did every night and how I planned my social activities to avoid eating in public. I began a slow descent into a hellish trap, from which there seemed to be no escape.

As my body became thinner, the scope of my life narrowed accordingly. I was living on the edge: the edge of life and death, in a world of punishment and denial. Any attempts at intervention from family and friends fell on

> **FAST FACT**
>
> Anorexics will generally avoid eating more than one hundred calories at a time. In fact, they will tend to stick to two-digit caloric values when making food choices.

While fitness can be a part of a healthy lifestyle, some people suffering from anorexia use exercise as a way to keep their weight down. (AP Images)

deaf ears. Anorexia had become my only friend, the only thing I could count on. It didn't matter that I was no longer in control; I just knew I had to follow the rules. The mere thought of deviation was too terrifying to even consider.

A Career in Fitness

Not surprisingly, a career in the fitness profession seemed well suited. It was an opportunity to burn more calories, while at the same time being in front of a mirror monitoring my body. I became a certified group-exercise instructor. As I gained experience, I quickly expanded my class schedule. Before long I was teaching 19 hours a week, while still consuming the minimum. My students and co-workers would occasionally comment on my appearance, but since I seemed to have so much energy, nobody really felt there was a problem.

By my late 30s, the eating disorder had such a stranglehold on me that my health began to decline. I fought to continue teaching, but in spring 2000 I was forced to enter a residential treatment center for around-the-clock care and monitoring. Acknowledging that I had to surrender control was terrifying. However, being fed through a tube was a defining moment for me. It was then I realized anorexia was winning the battle and I was going to die if things did not change.

After several months of treatment, I began the painful process of reentering my life—a life very different from the dangerous one I was accustomed to. This new life centered on consuming sufficient calories and severely curtailing exercise expenditures. At first, I was only allowed to teach two classes a week, which seemed like torture. Despite the treatment and counseling I received, on positive body image, nutrition and self-acceptance, old demons began to resurface. I found it difficult to adhere to my food plan if I wasn't allowed to exercise as much as I desired.

Focus on Weightlifting

In an effort to stay fit without teaching too many classes, I turned to weightlifting. At least, I reasoned, I could put on some lean muscle mass and keep my metabolism high.

The following year, I focused on strength training. Slowly I noticed an increase in energy. I could actually see some muscle definition on my previously stick-thin arms. Others noticed the changes as well and offered positive support instead of expressing concern as they had in the past.

As I continued lifting weights, my mindset began to change. Knowing I needed protein to feed my developing muscles, I kept track of what I ate and set calorie goals

Anorexia/Bulimia Progression Chart

1. Symptoms

Anorexia	Bulimia
Compulsive exercise	Preoccupation with eating food
Eating alone	Fatigue, apathy, irritability, anxiety, depression
Fatigue	Elimination of normal activities
Decreased scalp hair; thin, dry scalp	Gastrointestinal disorders
Emaciated appearance	Social isolation; distance from family and friends
Feelings of control over body	Dishonesty, lying, stealing food or money
Ridigity	Tooth damage, gum disease
Depression, apathy	Bingeing on high carbohydrate foods
Fear of food and gaining weight	Drug and alcohol abuse
Malnutrition	Laxative and diuretic abuse
Tyrannical mood swings	Mood swings
Sensitivity to cold	Chronic sore throat
Weakness (due to electrolyte imbalance)	Difficulty breathing and swallowing
Cardiac arrest	Anemia, hypokalemia
Denial of problem (sees self as fat)	Electrolytic imbalance
Joint pain (difficulty walking and sitting)	General ill health, chronic physical problems
Sleep disturbance	Suicidal tendencies or attempts

2. Recognition of Need for Help

3. Rehabilitation

Participation in psychiatric treatment plan
Acceptance of the illness
Ability to relax
Resumption of normal self-control and normal eating
Diminished fears
Relief from guilt and depression
Acceptance of psychiatric treatment plan

4. Recovery

Self-approval (not dependent on weight)
Achievement of personal goals in a wide range of activities
New friends and interests
Resumption of regular menstrual cycle
Acceptance of personal limitations
Enjoys eating food without guilt
Appreciation of spiritual values

5. Ongoing Support

Awareness and ease with life
More understanding of family
Respect for family and friends
Optimism
Improved self-image
Increased assertiveness
Honesty
Understanding of personal needs
Trust/openness

Source: Millville Public Schools. http://www.millville.org/Workshops_f/Camp_DISORDER/WHACKED/prog.htm.

each week. Instead of purposely skipping meals, I consumed protein shakes and protein bars in an effort to preserve the muscle I worked so hard to attain. To some, it probably seemed as though I traded one obsession for another. However, I am healthier now than I have been in years and enjoying the challenges of pushing my body in a stronger, more positive direction.

Recently I have been thinking of entering a bodybuilding or figure competition. This would require a lot of work in the gym, as well as ample and carefully planned nutrition. I have become devoted to this endeavor because it has made me aware of the need to feed my body, not just to survive, but to safely and adequately build muscle mass. And more importantly, for the first time, I accept what I see in the mirror rather than seeing a body needing to be punished into emaciation.

I have the power to affect change in my size through muscular strength and definition. The balance of power has shifted; this time I truly am in control, and the feeling is exhilarating. I will probably always be on the thinner side of "normal" in most people's eyes. However, I am no longer living on the edge. Rather, I am strong, confident and proudly taking up space.

A Woman Overcomes Bulimia

Diane Guernsey

This first-person account follows the constant cycle of self-hatred, binge eating, and induced vomiting of Diane Guernsey from beginning to end. Guernsey describes her teenage years when she believed that dieting and weight loss would solve her personal and social problems. However, the self-loathing never left her, and bulimia soon became an indispensable, yet secret, part of her life. As she went through a difficult move from her home and friends, Diane gained weight from excessive bingeing and began to see a psychotherapist. While she still could not bring herself to talk about the bulimia, even to her therapist, she continued to induce vomiting until she got involved in support groups and read books on women's eating disorders. In her late twenties, Guernsey finally shared her secret and successfully left bulimia behind her. Diane Guernsey writes for *Town & Country* magazine.

SOURCE: Diane Guernsey, "Bulimia: My Story: First, Dieting. Next, Years of Chronic Bulimia and Self-Loathing. How One Woman Turned Her Life Around Through Therapy and Her Own Inner Strength," *Town & Country*, v. 160, April, 2006. Copyright © 2006 Hearst Communications, Inc. All rights reserved. Reproduced by permission of the author.

It all began with the Grapefruit Diet [this diet includes grapefruits to enhance fat burning]. I was thirteen, growing up in Southern California. Little did I know that my first attempt at weight loss would set me on the path to bulimia—a path shadowed in shame and secrecy. Only now, more than twenty-five years later, can I look back and map the road I took through those shadows and back into health.

About the diet: I didn't understand what I was getting into. I thought I was entering a brave new world where, ten pounds thinner, I would become socially fluent and self-confident. This was a stretch: although I had good friends and hobbies I was passionate about, I was also shy, bookish and uncomfortable in my own skin—not exactly Popular Girl material. But I blamed all my social unease

Ipecac syrup is one method bulimics use to binge and purge food from their system. (**AP Images**)

on being slightly overweight—I was five foot eight and 140 pounds. If only that were different. . . .

Unfortunately, strict dieting led not to Nirvana but to an endless cycle: lose five pounds, gain five pounds; repeat. My fierce self-deprivation while following what my mother called "those crazy diets" also spurred me to binge eat rebelliously, so for two years my weight stayed put.

Introduced to Bulimia

Then a friend mentioned how some girls made themselves vomit to keep from gaining weight. I recoiled. Some time after that, though, I panicked and resorted to this bizarre weight-control method. My disgust with myself was outweighed only by the relief of having (as I thought) fended off fatness.

Gradually, purging became an integral part of my life—something I wasn't sure I could stop, and definitely something I couldn't tell anyone about. Looking in the mirror, I couldn't match that curvaceous but normal-looking fifteen-year-old girl with someone who would do such a monstrous thing. I shoved the knowledge deep down and tried to forget it.

Her Condition Gets Worse

Then, during my last year of high school, my life blew apart. My family moved across the country, whisking me away from my much-loved friends and into a small, snobbish school that had no place for me. Completely unprepared for the crushing sense of grief and loss, I began, blindly, furiously, to binge eat—a desperate, unconscious attempt to mute the crazy-making pain. In three months I gained forty pounds. Predictably, too, I began purging daily, often more than once, trying to undo the damage.

It was my worst nightmare come true. As agonizing as it was to feel totally out of control, it was even worse to feel consumed by self-loathing. No one else could possibly have despised me as much as I despised myself in those days.

I told no one about my purging. (My parents were horrified enough by my weight gain; I couldn't imagine what they'd say about this.) I learned that it had a medical name—bulimia—and that I was risking heart damage or worse. But I couldn't stop.

In my junior year at college, I used the money I'd earned working in the library to see a psychotherapist, who helped me grapple with some of my deepest fears—of leaving home, of social situations, of failing to find a place in the world—but he couldn't directly help me with my purging, because I felt too ashamed to tell him about it. Even so, the behavior subsided a bit.

FAST FACT

Of those who suffer from bulimia, about 50 percent will eventually recover, 30 percent will improve to an extent, and 20 percent will continue to exhibit the behavior and symptoms of bulimia.

Her Condition Improves

Emboldened by my success, I sought more help. During graduate school, I entered group therapy—and discovered that the other women there also struggled with food and eating. (Still, I didn't confide my own problem.) I attended workshops on women and food. I read Susie Orbach's *Fat Is a Feminist Issue* and Geneen Roth's *Feeding the Hungry Heart*, both of which explore how women use food, eating and weight to express (or suppress) painful feelings about their lives, relationships and gender roles. In a support group centered on this idea, I took my first tottery steps toward "no-fault," mindful eating: eating only when I was hungry, eating exactly what I wanted (be it dessert or steak), focusing on the food, stopping when I was full.

My bingeing and purging tapered off tremendously, and by grace or good luck, I had been spared bulimia's health ravages. But I still had more to learn. At twenty-eight, I embarked on intensive psychoanalysis, and, finally, I shared my secret.

Determining Your Body Mass Index (BMI)

The table below has already done the math and metric conversions. To use the table, find the appropriate height in the left-hand column. Move across the row to the given weight. The number at the top of the column is the BMI for that height and weight.

BMI (kg/m²)	19	20	21	22	23	24	25	26	27	28	29	30	35	40
Height (in.)	Weight (lb.)													
58	91	96	100	105	110	115	119	124	129	134	138	143	167	191
59	94	99	104	109	114	119	124	128	133	138	143	148	173	198
60	97	102	107	112	118	123	128	133	138	143	148	153	179	204
61	100	106	111	116	122	127	132	137	143	148	153	158	185	211
62	104	109	115	120	126	131	136	142	147	153	158	164	191	218
63	107	113	118	124	130	135	141	146	152	158	163	169	197	225
64	110	116	122	128	134	140	145	151	157	163	169	174	204	232
65	114	120	126	132	138	144	150	156	162	168	174	180	210	240
66	118	124	130	136	142	148	155	161	167	173	179	186	216	247
67	121	127	134	140	146	153	159	166	172	178	185	191	223	255
68	125	131	138	144	151	158	164	171	177	184	190	197	230	262
69	128	135	142	149	155	162	169	176	182	189	196	203	236	270
70	132	139	146	153	160	167	174	181	188	195	202	207	243	278
71	136	143	150	157	165	172	179	186	193	200	208	215	250	286
72	140	147	154	162	169	177	184	191	199	206	213	221	258	294
73	144	151	159	166	174	182	189	197	204	212	219	227	265	302
74	148	155	163	171	179	186	194	202	210	218	225	233	272	311
75	152	160	168	176	184	192	200	208	216	224	232	240	279	319
76	156	164	172	180	189	197	205	213	221	230	238	246	287	328

Body weight in pounds according to height and body mass index.

Source: Partnership for Healthy Weight Management. www.consumer.gov/weightloss/bmi.htm.

The relief was indescribable. My therapist calmly went about trying to understand the feelings, thoughts and events that had led to my behavior. Within months I stopped purging altogether.

Nowadays I've reached a basic equilibrium vis-a-vis food (well, most of the time—nobody's perfect). I truly love food, especially when I eat with attention. I also forget about food when I'm caught up in work; and, like most people, I sometimes overeat just because, or at holiday meals. The pain is gone, leaving room for freedom —even delight.

One moment when I knew I was truly getting well took place, in fact, at a *Town & Country* holiday party. Faced with a tray of fancy chocolate truffles, I neither flinched nor felt compelled to eat them all. I took one carefully in my fingers, nibbled it slowly, savoring every morsel down to the last, and was content.

A Young Girl Seeks Treatment for Anorexia

Sandy Fertman Ryan

In the following article writer Sandy Fertman Ryan reports on Jennifer, a thirteen-year-old girl who suffered a terrible loss with the death of her father. According to Ryan, although Jennifer had support from her mother and brother, the empty feeling within her grew to become anorexia. Jennifer became very self-conscious about her body, began to limit her eating, devised clever ways to hide the fact that she seldom ate, and wore baggy clothes. Ryan reports that because of the lack of food in her body, Jennifer became very moody, snapping at family and friends, was unable to sleep, and had no energy. Learning that anorexia had taken control of her, she checked into the Renfrew Center for Eating Disorders and received group therapy and medication. Ryan contends that the activities at the center made Jennifer realize how much she had to live for and how happy she could be once more. Sandy Fertman Ryan writes about weight and emotional issues in young girls for *Girls' Life* magazine.

SOURCE: Sandy Fertman Ryan, "Dying to be thin: even though she was pretty and popular, Jennifer only saw fat and ugly when she looked in the mirror. She shares with us the devastation of struggling with anorexia," *Girls' Life*, vol. 13, February-March 2007, pp. 52-55. Copyright 2007 © Monarch Avalon, Inc. Reproduced by permission.

My life seemed pretty perfect . . . until I was 7, that is. That's when my dad died of cancer. I was very close to him, especially because he knew he was ill and made an extra effort to spend time with me, my brother and sister. After he died, I was so sad but too young to really understand grief. My mom continued her work as a doctor, but she was around us a lot more after his death. Even so, I felt this enormous hole in my life that I couldn't explain.

Eating Me Up Inside

As I grew, so did that empty feeling. At 13, I gained a little weight and became very self-conscious about my body. Suddenly, I was hyper-aware of what I put into my mouth and was dieting for the first time in my life. I remember in middle school watching other girls eat whatever they wanted, like chocolate cake, and I would get so jealous!

Then there was high school, which kind of threw me for a loop. I was at a new school with kids I didn't know and, to top it off, my brother, who was like a father to me, would be graduating and moving away. I was pretty terrified.

Around that time, I radically changed my eating habits. I only allowed myself to eat a few specific foods, like cottage cheese and oatmeal, which I felt were "safe" since they wouldn't cause weight gain. I always skipped breakfast, but I ate "lunch" with friends in the cafeteria. My friends, who ate regular packed sandwiches and hot meals, sometimes asked why I was only eating a cereal bar. I always had an excuse, that I had wolfed a big breakfast or had eaten my lunch earlier. Since I always wore baggy clothes, no one really noticed how much weight I was losing.

Panicking about Food

Every night, my family ate dinner together. I had become so controlling about food that I was the one who cooked meals. I served everyone huge portions and gave myself tiny spoonfuls. If anyone even mentioned food to me or said, "Have some more," I panicked. In fact, I was even mean to them, which was weird, because I'd always been this nice, happy girl. I was suddenly edgy, and everyone had to tread lightly around me. Inside, I was miserable and confused. Controlling my food intake had become a complete priority in my life.

Instead of getting excited when my mom wanted to take us out to dinner, I'd get upset. I thought every single person in the restaurant was watching and trying to catch me not eating. So I would pick at my food and push it around my plate to make it look like I was eating.

My mom never forced me to eat. I don't think she ever realized how desperate I was to lose weight. It's likely she was in denial. It's hard to accept your daughter is letting herself wither away.

Split Personality?

Out of the blue, I had a horrible feeling that I'd developed multiple personalities. I didn't understand why I was so freaked and obsessed about food. I didn't know why I was angry and secretive. It was like another person had taken over. Weight loss had become my identity.

I almost always went to bed hungry and had anxiety about falling asleep. I was so weak that I believed if I slept, I would never wake up. Sometimes, I'd give in and binge, eating a whole pizza and a pie. Afterward I felt incredibly sick. Although I never vomited, I'd cry and cry —I hated myself for eating.

I had one friend I could talk to about my problem. I'd call him up to tell him I didn't know what was happening and that I didn't have any control over myself. He was supportive but, like all of my close friends, he never tried to convince me to do anything about it. I'm sure no one understood my problem was so serious. In fact, when I first stopped eating, I got tons of compliments. But within months, the positive comments had ceased because I looked awful.

By the end of freshman year, I'd lost half my body weight. It was horrible. I'd hate for any girl reading this to think, "Wow! That's what I want to do!" Truth is, I felt like I was drowning. My entire schedule was planned around food—when and what I'd eat, or not eat. Nothing else mattered. To ensure no one would discover my secret, I pulled straight A's to look like I was just busy.

Changes in Moods

My moods during this time were so up and down. I was really cranky at home, but I hid it from most of my friends. They truly believed I was happy. In reality, I was depressed and terrified. As I got thinner, my brother, sister and mom asked if I was all right. Still, they never tried to get me to eat. They knew I would snap at them if they did. It affected my closeness with them.

A few times, my mom sat me down to talk about my problem but, each time, I acted terrible toward her. Controlling my eating was more important to me than anything, even my relationship with my family and friends.

Eventually, I stopped seeing friends and only left the house to go to school. Before, I was very sociable and always out on the weekends. But I had become too weak, and I only wanted to use what energy I had to focus on not eating.

My brain was so starved that I honestly can't remember much about my freshman year, except the pain. My skin got extremely dry, and I grew hair all over my body because it didn't have enough fat and needed warmth. My period stopped after only three months, and I didn't know what was happening.

Yet, I was secretly proud of my skinniness. I got a sort of high from it, which is hard to describe. It's probably a

What Are the Symptoms of an Eating Disorder?

There are three major categories of eating disorders, Anorexia Nervosa, Bulimia Nervosa, and Binge Eating Disorder, all of which usually begin between early adolescence and early adulthood.

	Bulimia Nervosa	Binge Eating Disorder	Anorexia Nervosa
Do you have any of these symptoms?	Preoccupied with shape and weight	Preoccupied with shape and weight	Significantly underweight with a Body Mass Index* less than 17.5 or weight less than 85
	Bingeing: consuming an objectively large quantity of food while feeling a loss of control	Bingeing: consuming an objectively large quantity of food while feeling a loss of control	Intense fear of weight gain
	Have many "forbidden" foods	Have many "forbidden" foods	Absence of menstrual periods
	Try to go as long as possible without eating: skip meals; try "fad diets" to lose weight	Try to go as long as possible without eating: skip meals; try "fad diets" to lose weight	Self-starvation; try to go as long as possible without eating
	Eat in secret; hide food	Eat in secret; hide food	Extremely rigid diet excluding "forbidden foods"
	Feel disgusted about your body	Feel disgusted about your body	May include binges
	Check shape/weight with daily weighing, pinch body fat, try on "skinny" clothes	Check shape/weight with daily weighing, pinch body fat, try on "skinny" clothes	
	Disrupted social life because you avoid eating with others	Disrupted social life because you avoid eating with others	
	Purging: Vomit, laxative abuse, and/or excessive exercise after meals or binges	Feel ashamed about your eating and want to be more "in control"	
Who is affected?	2–5% of American population	2–5% of American population; 30% of overweight adults	Less than 1% of adolescent/ young adults

*Body Mass Index is a relationship between weight and height that is associated with body fat and heath risk.

Source: Millville Public Schools. http://www.millville.org/Workshops_f/Camp_DISORDER/WHACKED/prog.htm.

lot like a drug addiction, in which you just want more and more of that feeling. But by the end of the school year, I had an awful downward spiral. All that time I thought I'd been in control of my food, and I learned that it was in control of me.

Renfrew Center for Treatment

I knew I had to do something, so I went online to learn about eating disorders. When I read the symptoms of anorexia, I thought, "This can't be me!" I just wanted to be normal, but I knew I was losing my life. I talked to my mom and, together, we found a therapist for me.

I began weekly therapy sessions and was prescribed medications. My therapist tried to talk me into going to the Renfrew Center, a nearby inpatient facility for eating disorders, but I refused. Finally, after three months, I agreed to visit the center.

The day I went there was March 30 which, although I didn't realize it at the time, was the anniversary of my dad's death. I really didn't want to enter treatment because I knew I'd have to be admitted for seven weeks, and everyone at school would hear about it. But as soon as I got in the car with my mom after the visit, I said, "I think I need to go there." I went in the next day.

My treatment program turned out to be great. There were about 30 other girls there with eating disorders. We journaled, and had group and individual therapy sessions, all day long. We also had art, dance, coping and empowerment classes. It was just this amazing place where everyone worked together to get better. I felt cool being there because I was the youngest and could still remember a time when I was happy.

During my stay, I gained weight, which was emotionally tough to do. But, at the same time, it was a relief. I was determined to get my life back on track so, when they wanted me to eat, I ate. If I had refused to eat, they would have hospitalized me for tube-feeding.

My mom visited almost every night, giving me strength to get through it. My friends, brother, sister and even classmates I barely knew came to see me. It was awesome because not one person ever placed judgment on me. They just wanted me to know they cared.

A Full Life Once Again

I was released from Renfrew just before finishing ninth grade. I was so grateful because my brother had his graduation that weekend and I was able to be there. That had been a major motivation for me to do whatever I had to do to get better. After I got out, I had support from doctors and therapists. But I knew every day would be a challenge.

Looking back on my time at Renfrew, I think it was the best experience of my life. It was the first time I faced my problems and dealt with them instead of just stuffing them down. I learned so much about myself. I even learned to love myself, although that's still a work in progress. While I can't say I'm "cured," it is an ongoing daily process. But I haven't relapsed, even during stressful times. I haven't forgotten—and never want to forget—how I used to starve myself during trying times.

Now, I use my skills to deal with things in a more healthful way. My life is fairly normal, even though I'm still a big overachiever and get stressed. But I accept that about myself, and I know how to cope. My experience with anorexia was awful, but it definitely had a silver lining. I appreciate life more now—every millimeter of it. I've learned to be humane, to think things through and to be happy with myself. I truly believe my dad helped me through this rough spot. He showed me courage in the face of his illness, so I knew I could do it. And I definitely did not want to put my family through any more pain after they'd already endured so much.

If you have an eating problem, talk to someone about it right away. It's very difficult, if even possible, to get bet-

Self-image can impact the decision to lead a healthy lifestyle. (AP Images)

ter on your own. Although it's scary to think about, I probably would have died if I hadn't gone to treatment. That would have been a waste, especially seeing how my life has turned out. There are just too many things I want to do—go to college, get married, have kids, help people and even change the world! I couldn't do any of that if I hadn't gotten well. Now, I'm completely confident that I can—and will—accomplish my goals.

Thank Heaven.

GLOSSARY

amenorrhea	The absence or suppression of a menstrual period.
ana	Slang for anorexia or anorexic.
anorexia athletica	Excessive or compulsive exercise beyond a normal amount in an attempt to control weight. A person suffering from anorexia athletica no longer views exercise as fun, but sees it as a way to gain power and perfection.
anorexia nervosa	Meaning "nervous loss of appetite." An eating disorder in which a person intentionally limits food intake to the point of emaciation and malnutrition, typically due to an abnormal fear of gaining weight.
arrhythmia	A disorder in the heart's normal rate or rhythmic beating.
B&P	An abbreviation for bingeing and purging.
bigorexia	Also known as muscle dysmorphic disorder and the opposite of anorexia nervosa. A disorder in which individuals believe they are too thin, small, and frail even if they have normal muscle mass and body size.
binge-eating disorder	An eating disorder in which an individual consumes an abnormally large amount of food in one sitting on numerous occasions over a period of time.
body dysmorphic disorder	A disorder in which a person is preoccupied to the point of anxiety with his or her appearance, perceiving flaws in the face, hair, and skin.
body image	A person's subjective opinion about his or her physical appearance, such as shape, height, and weight. Body image is also based on the opinion and reactions of peers and family.

body mass index	A formula used to measure a person's body fat based on height, weight, and gender.
bulimia nervosa	Meaning "ravenous hunger." An eating disorder in which an individual binges on food then purges the food from the body by self-induced vomiting, through the use of laxatives and enemas, or with excessive exercise.
comorbid conditions	The presence of one or more physical and/or mental conditions coexisting in a patient in addition to the patient's primary disease or disorder.
compulsive eating disorder	Also known as compulsive overeating, it is an eating disorder in which an individual feels addicted to food, eating more food and eating more often than normal. The individual uses food to overcome feelings of inadequacy, shame, and loneliness.
cynorexia	Meaning "hunger like that of a starved dog," a disorder in which an individual suffers from a voracious appetite and is possessed by the thought of food, then overeats and purges the food, usually by vomiting.
dental caries	Also known as cavities, dental caries are holes in teeth. People with bulimia are especially susceptible to cavities because the stomach acid from excessive vomiting can damage teeth.
eating disorder	An illness in which an individual develops harmful eating patterns, typically by eating either too little or too much. Anorexia nervosa, bulimia nervosa, and binge eating are the most common types of eating disorders. A combination of genetic factors, environmental situations, and mental health issues like depression are causes of eating disorders.
electrolyte imbalance	A physical condition in which the body has a low level of certain vital chemicals, such as sodium, potassium, magnesium, and calcium, which in severe cases can lead to dehydration, cardiac arrest, organ failure, and death. People with bulimia tend to suffer electrolyte imbalance due to excessive vomiting.
emetic	A drug or substance, administered orally or by injection, that induces vomiting. People with bulimia use emetics to purge food from the body.

enema	The injection of liquid into the rectum for the purpose of evacuating the bowel. This technique is used by bulimics to purge food from the body.
hyperorexia	A synonym for bulimia.
hypoglycemia	An abnormal decrease of glucose, or sugar, in the blood.
ketosis	A medical condition characterized by an abnormal increase of ketones, or organic compounds, in the body, typically brought on by starvation, alcoholism, and diabetes.
Mallory-Weiss tear	A tear in the mucous membrane where the esophagus connects to the stomach that causes bleeding. A common cause of the tear is long-term vomiting or coughing.
mia	Slang for bulimia or bulimic.
night-eating syndrome	An eating disorder in which an individual usually foregoes breakfast and eats most of his or her calories late in the day, in the evening, or during the night.
obesity	An excessive amount of body fat, specifically a body mass index of more than 25 percent for men and 30 percent for women.
obsessive-compulsive disorder	A psychiatric disorder in which an individual participates in unwanted thoughts or obsessions and repetitive and compulsive behavior to the point of performing rituals to alleviate the feelings of anxiety.
orthorexia nervosa	Meaning "correct appetite." An eating disorder in which a person obsesses on the "purity" of food, such as organic food or food found in health food stores, as well as the food's purchase and preparation.
osteoporosis	A condition characterized by thinning bones, a decrease in bone mass, or porous or brittle bones that often leads to fractures. Osteoporosis, often caused by the lack of calcium and protein, is a common complication of anorexia and bulimia.
pica	An eating disorder in which a person craves nonfood items such as dirt, clay, crayons, chalk, hair, and paint chips.

polyphagia	A condition in which a person has the absence of a feeling of fullness and experiences excessive hunger which leads to devouring an abnormally large amount of food in one sitting.
remission	The abatement or absence of the symptoms of a disease for a period of time.
substance abuse	The misuse of illegal drugs or alcohol leading to impairment and lack of judgment.
thinspiration	A slang term used for photographs, poems, very thin models, or other things used to inspire and encourage young women to lose a lot of weight and become exceptionally thin.
trigger	A stimulus that initiates a physiological process or reflex behavior or return to previous habits.

CHRONOLOGY

A.D. **200–400** Latin writings by Aulus Gellius and Sextus Pompeius Festus describe the conditions of bulimia.

1200–1500 During the medieval era, many women practice "holy anorexia," starving themselves to achieve mystical divinity and a closer relationship with God.

1398 In the encyclopedia *De Proprietatibus Rerum* (On the Order of Things), English writer and translator John Trevisa describes "true boulimus" as a preoccupation with food followed by vomiting.

1689 In his *Phisiologia: A Treatise on Consumption*, British physician Richard Morton (1637–1698) describes the condition of anorexia nervosa.

1694 Morton reports the first case of anorexia in a sixteen-year-old man.

1797 Bulimia is listed in the *Encyclopedia Britannica*.

1859 French physician Louis Victor Marce (1828–1864) was the first to publish a clinical account of a patient with anorexia nervosa.

1873 British physician Sir William Withey Gull (1819–1890) coins the term "anorexia nervosa" in a scientific paper, which he presents at a meeting of the Clinical Society of London, and which he publishes in 1874.

1873   French physician and psychiatrist Ernest-Charles Lasègue (1816–1883) of the University of Paris writes of anorexia in his *L'Anorexie Hysterique*.

1932   In a paper for the German Psychoanalytic Society, Russian physician Moshe Wulff describes cases of eating disorders in women who binge eat, fast, vomit, and exhibit hypersomnia and irritability.

1932   The *New England Journal of Medicine* publishes the first photograph of a girl suffering from anorexia.

1945   In post–World War II, bulimia becomes more common when food is plentiful and when society begins to admire slender celebrities.

1967   British model Twiggy (Lesley Hornby), at 5 feet 7 inches and 92 pounds, initiates a trend toward excessive thinness.

1976   American counselor Marlene Boskind-White, PhD, uses the word bulimarexia to describe women of normal weight who alternate between bingeing and fasting.

1978   Psychologist Hilde Bruch publishes *The Golden Cage*, a culmination of nearly thirty years of clinical experience with seventy patients suffering from anorexia nervosa.

1979   British professor Gerald Russell of Royal Free Hospital in London uses the term "bulimia nervosa" to recognize a variant syndrome of anorexia nervosa.

1980   The American Psychiatric Association recognizes bulimia nervosa as an autonomous eating disorder.

1983   Popular singer Karen Carpenter dies from heart failure brought on by anorexia. Her death makes the public more aware of the illness.

1985   The Renfrew Center in Philadelphia is the first freestanding facility dedicated exclusively to treating eating disorders.

1986   Ruth H. Strigel-Moore, Lisa R. Silberstein, and Judith Rodin publish the article "Toward an Understanding of Risk Factors for Bulimia" in the *American Psychologist*, saying that female socialization is a contributing factor in bulimia.

1996   Walter Kaye begins the first study, supported by the Price Foundation, to find a genetic link to eating disorders.

2000   The National Institute of Mental Health sponsors the Prevention of Eating Disorders Roundtable.

ORGANIZATIONS TO CONTACT

The editors have compiled the following list of organizations concerned with the issues debated in this book. The descriptions are derived from materials provided by the organizations. All have publications or information available for interested readers. The list was compiled on the date of publication of the present volume; the information provided here may change. Be aware that many organizations take several weeks or longer to respond to inquiries, so allow as much time as possible.

Academy for Eating Disorders
60 Revere Dr.,
Suite 500
Northbrook, IL
60062-1577
(847) 498-4274
info@aedweb.org
www.aedweb.org

An international transdisciplinary professional organization that promotes research, treatment, and prevention of eating disorders by providing education, training, and a forum for collaboration and dialogue.

American Academy of Child and Adolescent Psychiatry (AACAP)
3615 Wisconsin Ave. NW
Washington, DC
20016-3007
(202) 966-7300
communications@aacap.org
www.aacap.org

The AACAP is composed of child and adolescent psychiatrists who actively research, evaluate, diagnose, and treat psychiatric disorders.

American Dietetic Association (ADA)
120 South Riverside Plaza, Suite 2000
Chicago, IL 60606-6995
(800) 877-1600
www.eatright.org

The ADA is the nation's largest organization of food and nutrition professionals who promote optimal nutrition, health, and well-being. The Web site provides food and nutrition information through fact sheets, brochures, and other information.

American Psychiatric Association
1000 Wilson Blvd., Suite 1825
Arlington, VA 22209-3901
(703) 907-7300
apa@psych.org
www.psych.org

A medical specialty society that works to ensure humane care and effective treatment for all persons with mental disorders.

Anorexia Nervosa and Related Eating Disorders (ANRED)
PO Box 5102
Eugene, OR 97405
(541) 344-1144
www.anred.com

Anorexia Nervosa and Related Eating Disorders (ANRED) is a nonprofit organization that provides information about anorexia nervosa, bulimia nervosa, binge-eating disorder, and other food and weight disorders. The ANRED Web site includes forums for discussion, research studies, and clinical trials, as well as additional resources.

Eating Disorders Anonymous
18233 N. 16th Way
Phoenix, AZ 85022
www.eatingdisorder
sanonymous.org

Eating Disorders Anonymous is an online fellowship of individuals who share their experiences and help others to recover from their eating disorders. The Web site includes workbooks, brochures, and recovery stories.

Eating Disorders Coalition
611 Pennsylvania Ave. SE, #423
Washington, DC 20003-4303
(202) 543-9570
mlerro@eatingdisor ders coalition.org
www.eatingdisorder scoalition.org

The coalition's mission is to advance the federal recognition of eating disorders as a public health priority and to increase resources for research, education, prevention, and improved training. The Eating Disorders Coalition Web site includes links to reports and information resources.

Harris Center at Massachusetts General Hospital
Two Longfellow Place, Suite 200
Boston, MA 02114
(617) 726-8470
dherzog@partners.org
www.harriscenter mgh.org

The Harris Center is dedicated to expanding knowledge about eating disorders, their detection, treatment, and prevention, and promoting the healthy development of children, women, and all at risk.

National Association for Mental Illness (NAMI)
Colonial Place Three
2107 Wilson Blvd., Suite 300
Arlington, VA 22201-3042
(800) 950-6264
www.nami.org

The National Association for Mental Illness is the nation's largest grassroots mental health organization. NAMI is dedicated to improving the lives of persons with mental illness and their families. NAMI publishes the magazine *Advocate* as well as an e-newsletter and numerous press releases.

National Association of Anorexia Nervosa and Associated Disorders (ANAD)
PO Box 7
Highland Park, IL 60035
(847) 831-3438
www.anad.org

ANAD offers hotline counseling, operates an international network of support groups for people with eating disorders and their families, and provides referrals to health care professionals who treat eating disorders. It produces a quarterly newsletter and information packets and organizes national conferences and local programs. All ANAD services are provided free of charge.

National Eating Disorders Association (NEDA)
603 Steward St., Suite 803
Seattle, WA 98101-1264
(800) 931-2237
info@NationalEatingD isorders.org
www.edap.org

NEDA is the largest not-for-profit organization in the United States working to prevent eating disorders and provide treatment referrals to those suffering from anorexia, bulimia, and binge-eating disorder.

National Eating Disorders Screening Program
One Washington St., Suite 304
Wellesley Hills, MA 02481
(781) 239-0071
smhinfo@mental healthscreening.org
www.mentalhealth screening.org

Provides in-person and online programs for eating disorders implemented by local clinicians at mental health facilities, hospitals, primary care offices, social service agencies, colleges and universities, workplaces, schools, and the military.

National Institute of Mental Health (NIMH)
Public Information and Communications Branch
6001 Executive Blvd., Rm. 8184, MSC 9663
Bethesda, MD 20892-9663
(866) 615-6464
nimhinfo@nih.gov
www.nimh.nih.gov

NIMH aims to reduce the burden of mental and behavioral disorders through research on the mind, brain, and behavior, and to generate research that will transform prevention of and recovery from mental disorders. NIMH offers free, easy-to-read fact sheets, pamphlets, and booklets that are available in both English and Spanish.

U.S. Department of Health and Human Services
Substance Abuse and Mental Health Services Administration
PO Box 42557
Washington, DC 20015
(800) 789-2647
http://mentalhealth.samhsa.gov

The National Mental Health Information Center provides information about mental health via a toll-free telephone number, its Web site, and more than six hundred publications, including the SAMHSA News, a quarterly newsletter. The Web site also provides access to the National Library of Medicine and the National Academies Press.

FOR FURTHER READING

Books

Pamela Carlton, and Deborah Ashin, *Take Charge of Your Child's Eating Disorder: A Physician's Step-by-Step Guide to Defeating Anorexia and Bulimia.* New York: Marlowe, 2006.

Laura Goodman, and Mona Villapiano, *Eating Disorders: The Journey to Recovery Workbook.* New York: Brunner-Routledge, 2001.

Lori Gottlieb, *Stick Figure: A Diary of My Former Self.* New York: Simon & Schuster, 2001.

Lauren Greenfield, and Joan Jacobs, Brumberg, *Thin.* San Francisco: Chronicle, 2006.

Carlos, M. Grilo, *Eating and Weight Disorders.* New York: Psychology, 2006.

Michelle Heffner, et al., *The Anorexia Workbook: How to Accept Yourself, Heal Your Suffering, and Reclaim Your Life.* Oakland, CA: New Harbinger, 2004.

Aimee Liu, *Gaining: The Truth About Life After Eating Disorders.* New York: Warner, 2007.

Richard Maisel, and David Epston, *Biting the Hand That Starves You: Inspiring Resistance to Anorexia/Bulimia.* New York: Norton, 2004.

Dianne Neumark-Sztainer, *I'm, Like, SO Fat! Helping Your Teen Make Healthy Choices about Eating and Exercise in a Weight-Obsessed World!* New York: Guilford, 2005.

Michael Strober, *Just a Little Too Thin: How to Pull Your Child Back from the Brink of an Eating Disorder.* New York: Da Capo, 2005.

Periodicals

"Anorexia, Bulimia Prove Gene Related," *USA Today*, October 2006.

"An Overview of Pro-ana Websites," *Eating Disorders Review,* September/October 2006.

Bruce Bower, "Wasting Away," *Science News,* June 17, 2006.

Jennifer Brunning Brown, et al., "An Evaluation of an Internet-Delivered Eating Disorder Prevention Program for Adolescents and Their Parents," *Journal of Adolescent Health,* October 2004.

Tessa DeCarlo, "Eating Disorders," *A.D.A.M.,* 2005.

_____, "Eating Issues Becoming More Common Among Men," *Mental Health Weekly,* October 18, 2004.

_____, "When Diets Turn Deadly," *Ladies' Home Journal,* June 2005.

Jeff Evans, "Factors Driving Anorexia, Bulimia Are Complex: About Two-thirds of Eating Disorder Patients Have Comorbid Diagnosis of Anxiety or Depression," *Clinical Psychiatry News,* December 2006.

Angela Favaro, et al., "Perinatal Factors and the Risk of Developing Anorexia Nervosa and Bulimia Nervosa," *Archives of General Psychiatry,* January 2006.

Barbara Feder Ostrov, "Health Plans Leave Anorexics Struggling: Insurers Often Pay Only Treatment of Eating Disorders," *San Jose Mercury News,* February 13, 2007.

Naomi Field, "My Story: Dying to Be Thin," *Woman's Day,* March 7, 2006.

Debbe Geiger, "Can You Catch an Eating Disorder Online?" *Ladies' Home Journal,* January 2006.

Arline Kaplan, "Exploring the Gene-Environment Nexus in Anorexia, Bulimia," *Psychiatric Times,* August 2004.

Gail McVey, and Manuela Ferrari, "Dieting and Children," *Pediatrics for Parents,* 2005.

DianneNeumark-Sztainer, "Teenagers at Risk for Range of Health-Threatening Weight Problems, from Obesity to Anorexia: Can Parents Help Avoid One Without Encouraging the Other?" *Ascribe Newswire Health,* June 14, 2005.

Sean Poulter, "Designers Should Face Court over Size-Zero Girls," *Daily Mail*, February 5, 2007.

_____, "Promotion of Healthy Weight-Control Practices in Young Athletes," *Pediatrics*, December 2005.

Susan M. Sawyer, "Dieting in Adolescence: Not to Be Taken Lightly," *Nutridate*, July 2004.

Vicki Sheff-Cahan, "A Daughter's Secret," *People*, January 29, 2007.

Jim Shelton, "Looking Back Now: Yale Grad Has a Greater Understanding of Her Eating Disorder," *New Haven Register*, February 15, 2007.

Sora Song, "Starvation on the Web," *Time*, July 18, 2005.

Polly Sparling, "Empty Inside," *Current Health 2*, January 2005.

Karen Springen, "Battle of the Binge," *Newsweek*, February 19, 2007.

_____, "Sites Walk a Thin Line," *Newsweek*, December 18, 2006.

Erik Strand, "A New Eating Disorder?" *Psychology Today*, September/October 2004.

_____, "Study: Childhood Anxiety Can Lead to Eating Disorders," *Mental Health Weekly*, December 13, 2004.

_____, "Surfing Pro-eating Disorder Websites," *Pediatric Alert*, December 28, 2006.

_____, "The Skinny on Models," *Current Events*, January 8, 2007.

Susan Woods, "Untreated Recovery from Eating Disorders," *Adolescence*, Summer 2004.

D. Blake Woodside, et al., "Predictors of Premature Termination of Inpatient Treatment for Anorexia Nervosa," *American Journal of Psychiatry*, December 2004.

INDEX